ISRAEL IN ANTIQUITY

ISRAEL IN ANTIQUITY:

This exhibition has been made possible by a grant from the
Dorot Foundation and through the gift of the
Betty and Max Ratner Collection of Antiquities.

Funds for this catalogue have been provided by a gift from
Mr. and Mrs. Max and Betty Ratner

FROM DAVID TO HEROD
THE JEWISH MUSEUM / NEW YORK

by Andrew S. Ackerman and Susan L. Braunstein, Exhibition curators

Essays by Eric Meyers and Arielle Kozloff

PHOTO CREDITS:

All color and black and white photographs by Graydon Wood with the following exceptions:
 Institute of Archaeology, University of London (p. 34)
Jewish Quarter Excavations (p. 77)
Oriental Institute (#2)
Ratner Collection (#5, 30, 47, 48, 61, 68, 87, 123, 138)
The University Museum, University of Pennsylvania (#1)
Yale University Art Gallery (#110, 123, 124)

LENDERS TO THE EXHIBITION

Daniel M. Friedenberg, New York
Hebrew Union College/Skirball Museum
The Metropolitan Museum of Art
The Newark Museum
The Oriental Institute, University of Chicago
Mr. and Mrs. Norbert Schimmel, New York
The Joseph Ternbach Collections
The University Museum, University of Pennsylvania
Yale Babylonian Collection
Yale University Art Gallery

Design Consultant: Albert Squillace
Produced and Prepared by Layla Productions, Inc., New York
Typography by Precision Typographers
Printed and Bound by Murray Printing, Inc.
Exhibition Designed by Leone Design, Inc., New York

Copyright © 1982 by The Jewish Museum, 1109 Fifth Avenue, New York, New York 10028, under the auspices of The Jewish Theological Seminary of America.

ISBN: 0-87334-0159
LCC: 82-10077

TABLE OF CONTENTS

PERIOD	DATE	HISTORICAL EVENTS AND FIGURES	LEVELS AT LACHISH	AREAS OF JERUSALEM OCCUPIED
	640 CE			
BYZANTINE				
	330 CE			
ROMAN Late		Early Synagogues		
	180 CE			
Middle	70 CE	Bar-Kokhba Revolt Destruction of the Temple		City of David
Early		Jesus Herod the Great		Upper City and Northern Quarter
	63 CE			
HASMONEAN				City of David Upper City
	164 BCE	Judah Maccabee		
HELLENISTIC				City of David
	330 BCE	Alexander the Great		
PERSIAN		Ezra Nehemiah	I	City of David
	586 BCE	Exile		
IRON AGE		Josiah	II	
	700 BCE		III	
IA II C		Hezekiah	IV	
	800 BCE			
	928 BCE	Division of the Kingdom		Upper City
IA II A–B		Solomon		City of David
	1000 BCE	David	V	Temple Mount
IA I				
	1200 BCE	Joshua		
LATE BRONZE AGE LB II		Exodus	VI	Jebusite city on
	1400 BCE			southern hill
LB I			VII	
	1550 BCE			
MIDDLE BRONZE AGE MB II C		Patriarchs?	VIII	Jebusite city on southern hill
	1750 BCE			
MB II A–B				
	2000 BCE			
MB I				
	2200 BCE			

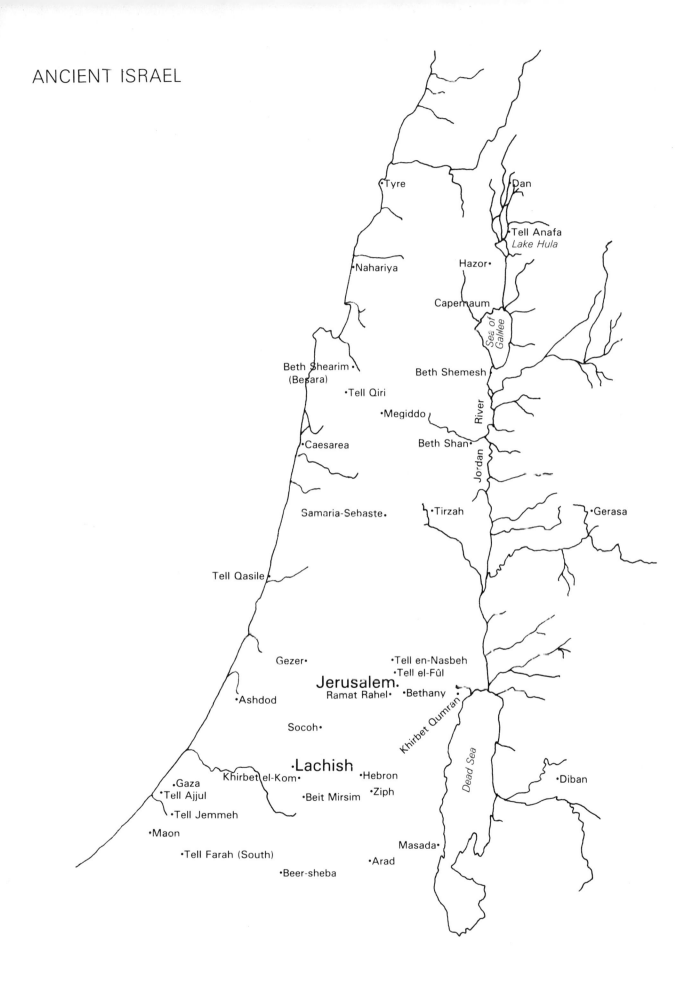

ANCIENT ISRAEL

•Tyre

Dan•

•Tell Anafa
Lake Hula

•Nahariya   Hazor•

Capernaum

Sea of Galilee

Beth Shearim•   Beth Shemesh•
(Besara)

•Tell Qiri

•Megiddo

•Caesarea   Beth Shan•

Samaria-Sebaste•   •Tirzah   •Gerasa

Tell Qasile•

Gezer•   •Tell en-Nasbeh
                 •Tell el-Fûl

Jerusalem•
Ramat Rahel• •Bethany
•Ashdod

Socoh•

•Lachish

Khirbet el-Kom• •Hebron
•Gaza
•Tell Ajjul   •Beit Mirsim •Ziph   •Diban
•Tell Jemmeh

•Maon

•Tell Farah (South)   Masada•
                 •Arad
•Beer-sheba

Jordan River

Khirbet Qumran

Dead Sea

ACKNOWLEDGEMENTS

When we began to think about the possibility of a new installation of The Jewish Museum's archaeology collection in the fall of 1980, we were faced with innumerable ways of organizing the material and presenting it to the public. The present concept was a product of the thoughts of many people to whom we are indebted for helping us to focus our ideas and for their constant support.

Our first vote of thanks goes to Betty and Max Ratner, whose generous donation of their collection of antiquities to the Museum was instrumental in shaping the scope of this exhibition. In this regard, we wish to thank Arielle Kozloff, Associate Curator in charge of Ancient Art at the Cleveland Museum, who originally catalogued the Ratner Collection, and who was always available for consultation. Without the guidance of Joy Ungerleider-Mayerson at the beginning of this project, and her continued help while in the United States and in Israel, we would have undoubtedly taken many a wrong turn. Joan Rosenbaum, the new director of The Jewish Museum, brought her endless energy and concern to the exhibition; we are thankful for her vision and for her faith in us. To Dr. Vivian B. Mann a special note of thanks is due for her conceptual input, scholarly insight, and invaluable assistance in obtaining objects for the exhibition. Special thanks are extended to Ruth Dolkart, Museum Administrator, whose involvement insured the completion of both the exhibition and the catalogue.

Anne Donadeo, Research Assistant for the Catalogue, provided the research for many of the objects in preparation for the entries and helped in the coordination of the exhibition, frequently above and beyond the call of duty. Keren Whitman, an intern from the Jewish Theological Seminary, assisted with research and coordination.

Among our colleagues in Israel who helped bring this exhibition to fruition, we must thank Yaakov Meshorer of The Israel Museum, who greatly assisted in obtaining objects for the exhibition, and Nahman Avigad of the Hebrew University, David Ussishkin of Tel Aviv University and Ruth Hestrin of The Israel Museum for their advice and cooperation. Gratitude is also expressed to our colleagues from other institutions who helped facilitate the loans: William Hallo (Yale Babylonian Collection), Samuel Wolff (The Oriental Institute), Susan Auth (The Newark Museum), Susan Matheson (Yale University Art Gallery), James Sauer (The University Museum) and Holly Pitman (The Metropolitan Museum of Art). Information on individual objects was provided by Roger Bagnall, Linda Roccos, Neil Goldman, Steve Nicklas, David Hendin and Corethea Qualls.

We thank Lucian Leone, exhibition designer, for his personal warmth and interest in the project, and extend great appreciation to his assistant, Michael Batista. Our colleagues at The Jewish Museum all deserve credit for the completion of the exhibition, especially Philip Goldman, Norman Kleeblatt, Anne Driesse, Karen Wilson, Judith Siegal, Phyllis Greenspan, Sharon Makover, Rita Feigenbaum and Charles Brand.

A. S. A.
S. L. B.

FOREWORD

The opening of the exhibition *Israel in Antiquity* and the publication of this catalogue mark the confluence of two important gifts to The Jewish Museum, as well as a major step in the development of the Museum's exhibition and education programs. The gift of a fund for archaeology from the Dorot Foundation in 1980 provided us with the means to continue to document and interpret the formative era of Jewish history through a new installation of biblical archaeology. This installation received additional impetus with the donation of the Betty and Max Ratner Collection of Antiquities to the Museum in 1981. The Ratner Collection augmented the Museum's holdings particularly in the period of the Second Temple, allowing us to elucidate two important time periods in the development of Jewish culture, the Iron Age and the Second Temple Period.

The theme of the new exhibition is the exploration, via two sites, of the religion, home life and political environment of the period from 1000 BCE to 70 CE. Our objective is to provide the visitor with a point of departure for the later Jewish history explored in the various temporary exhibitions in the Museum, and also to provide background for understanding the Judaica in the Museum's collection.

We are most grateful to Joy Ungerleider-Mayerson, the former Director of the Museum, both for her generosity and the role she played in initiating the subject of biblical archaeology into the Museum's program. Mr. and Mrs. Max Ratner are to be thanked profusely, not only for their wonderful gift, but also for their contribution toward the publication of the exhibition catalogue.

The Museum's own holdings have been supplemented in the exhibition with loans from private New York collections and other museums for to whom we are most appreciative. Extraordinary thanks are due to the two curators of the exhibition, Susan Braunstein, Assistant Curator of Judaica, and Andrew Ackerman, Director of Education, whose scholarship, sensitivity and prodigious efforts have combined to create an exhibition which the Museum presents with pride. The Board of Trustees of the Museum are also thanked for their support and enthusiasm for the project, and their recognition of its importance to the Museum. Together, the staff, Board, consultants and donors have worked to produce an exhibition which highlights the unique role played by The Jewish Museum.

Joan Rosenbaum
Director

Introduction

From the outset of the planning of *Israel in Antiquity* it was our conviction that this exhibition, as a permanent installation at The Jewish Museum, needed to explore the culture of ancient Israel, and not merely to present objects in a vacuum. Because the biblical period witnessed the formation of Jewish religion and tradition, we felt it necessary to focus on those aspects of the ancient culture that contributed to the development and perseverance of Jewish culture.

Much of the information required to interpret the culture of ancient Israel is the product of a combination of historical, theological and archaeological studies. Biblical archaeology is unique in that its course over the past century has been so heavily influenced by the study of the Bible. In many instances, archaeological excavations and the interpretation of objects have emanated from biblical studies and have not proceeded as an independent discipline.

In contrast to this legacy, the exhibition *Israel in Antiquity* was conceived and designed to let the archaeological evidence speak for itself. Biblical references and correlations are utilized as a secondary means of evidence when they help to clarify the archaeological data, or when, as in the case of religious practices in the Temple, archaeological sources are silent.

We decided to begin the exhibition with the tenth century BCE, when the combination of biblical narrative, archaeological remains, and later historical sources indicate that Israel was established as a new political entity. Indeed, it is only with the establishment of the state of Israel under David and Solomon that archaeologists can be fairly certain that excavated remains reflect Israelite society. While the beginnings of Jewish history reach back to the time of the patriarchal period, we eschewed making any correlation between remains from the Bronze Age and the biblical periods of the Patriarchs, the Exodus, and the Judges. This is not to refute the historicity of those people or events, but to underscore the difficulties inherent in attempting to date and identify these individuals and specific events in the archaeological remains of the Canaanite culture.

In order to carry out this ambitious goal we concentrated on three interrelated approaches to the exhibition. First, we wished to discern those aspects of ancient Israelite society that were instrumental in the development and perseverence of Jewish culture during and after the biblical period. Our second aim was to highlight the evolution of ancient Israelite culture over the millennium from David to Herod and to avoid the homogenization of the whole biblical period into one view of "life in biblical times." Thirdly, we felt that it was necessary to exhibit objects in the cultural context within which they were used, insofar as can be reconstructed from the archaeological record.

In analyzing ancient Israelite society from both the biblical and archaeological records, it seemed to us that three threads run through both biblical and Diaspora Judaism,[1] threads that have been strong enough to maintain a continuous tradition for three thousand years: the religion; the strong traditional role of home life (including those Jewish rituals and customs performed by the family) and the sense of national identity with its spiritual center in Jerusalem. These three social institutions—religion, the home and the state—became the thematic focus of the exhibition and one of the bases for our selection of objects.

Although archaeologists cannot hope to unearth the thoughts and ideologies that produced the artifact, we can hope to trace the manifestations of the beliefs and behavior of ancient people by studying the types of objects they did and did not produce, their style and technology, and where and how they were used. Aided by the information extracted from these remains and from textual sources, we can attempt to reconstruct ancient society. However, the extent to which we can make social reconstructions is limited by the types of analysis and data recovery presently available.

In order to portray a sense of dynamicism in the material culture of the first millennium BCE, *Israel In Antiquity* focuses on the home, religion and the Israelite state of the Iron Age (1000–586 BCE) and the Second Temple Period (515 BCE–70 CE). These two periods are separated not only by the cataclysmic event of the Exile but also by a shift in the seat of world power from the ancient Near East to the Aegean. By contrasting these two periods it is hoped that both continuity and discontinuity in material culture and social institutions will be highlighted. In both of these time periods, everyday life varied significantly from region to region and from the city to the countryside. Because most extensive excavations in Israel have been conducted on large tells (mounds) that are the remains of ancient cities, most archaeological evidence for both time periods reflects conditions as they were in the cities. We have selected two of these cities, Lachish of the Iron Age and Jerusalem of the Second Temple Period as type sites of their respective times. Through an examination of the evidence for home life, religious practices, and the functioning of the state in each of these cities, we hope to present a paradigm of how the three institutions selected may have functioned for a large part of the population. The selection of these sites was facilitated by three factors: one, the presence of a large amount of material in the Jewish Museum collection from the excavation of Lachish in the 1930s; two, the donation of the Betty and Max Ratner Collection, which increased our holdings of material from the Hellenistic and Roman Periods, and three, the recent excavations at both Lachish and Jerusalem that have revealed remarkable and intriguing insights into the three aspects of life.

The third goal of this exhibition, to present objects in their cultural contexts, resulted in the reconstruction of two excavated areas from Lachish, a sanctuary and a home, and of a Herodian home from Jerusalem. It is hoped that these reconstructions will emphasize the importance of archaeological provenance and will help visitors better understand ritual and domestic life in ancient Israel.

The exhibition does not conclude with the destruction of the Second Temple in 70 CE, the event that marked the end of the period of ancient Jewish culture centered in Israel. For the destruction of the Temple and dispersion of the Jewish population also marks the beginning of a new era, the Diaspora, when major transformations in the religious and political status of Israel enabled the Jewish culture to continue in a new form. The exhibition's Epilogue, "Early Synagogues and the Development of Jewish Symbols," briefly introduces the rise of small and large Jewish communities throughout much of the known world. In many of these communities, the synagogue assumed a new role, evolving from a local meeting place to a place of communal worship and finally as a central social and religious institution for Diaspora Jews. But the Temple and the land of Israel were far from forgotten, as evidenced by the now distinctly Jewish symbols on both ceremonial and domestic objects that began to appear in the Roman Period. The Epilogue also serves as a bridge between the rest of the Jewish Museum's collection, whose ceremonial objects evidence the diversity of form given to early Jewish symbols by subsequent generations.

Israel in Antiquity, therefore, is not an exhibition of a fossilized culture from antiquity, but a presentation of a living, thriving culture that has direct links to today's Jewish culture throughout the world.

The Jewish Museum Archaeological Collection: A Brief History

The archaeological collection of The Jewish Museum consists almost exclusively of objects from ancient Israel, beginning with some Paleolithic material but concentrating in the so-called "Biblical Period" from the second millennium BCE through the first centuries CE. The collection is under the aegis of the Judaica Department, which also oversees the most comprehensive collection of Jewish ceremonial objects in the western hemisphere. The inclusion of archaeological material with ceremonial objects reflects the Museum's recognition of these ancient artifacts as manifestations of Jewish religion and cultural traditions from its earliest phases, just as modern ceremonial objects mirror today's Jewish traditions.

The early core of the archaeological collection was housed at The Jewish Theological Seminary until 1947, when the Museum was moved to its present site in the Warburg mansion. The early archaeological collection was obtained primarily from two major collectors of Judaica, whose interest in antiquities focused primarily on objects with Jewish symbols, rather than on unadorned artifacts. The first such collection to be acquired was that of Hadji Ephraim Benguiat and his brothers, a family of Turkish Jews who purchased objects in the Mediterranean area, Europe and the United States in the late 1800s. Their Judaica collection was obtained by The Jewish Museum in 1925, and the archaeological objects were limited primarily to clay oil lamps of the Byzantine Period, bearing Jewish symbols. The second major collector of Judaica was Dr. Harry G. Friedman, who from 1941 to his death in 1965 gave the Museum over 6,000 objects.

A new dimension was added to the archaeological collection with the donation in 1948 of a comprehensive series of coins, medals and tokens by Samuel Friedenberg. Included in this series was a group of ancient coins from Israel dating from ca. 500 BCE to 500 CE, originally in the Harry J. Stein collection. Other smaller donations and purchases, mostly of pottery, extended the chronological and typological range of the Museum's collection to the Middle Bronze and the Iron Ages. However, the first significant increase in the depth and range of the archaeological collection occurred in 1973 when Joy Ungerleider-Mayerson, then Director of the Museum, negotiated the acquisition of a group of nearly 600 excavated pieces from ancient Israel from the New York University Classics Department. These pieces were originally part of the collection of H. Dunscombe Colt, who participated in a number of excavations in Israel in the earlier part of this century. It was customary at that time to reward donors to excavations with a portion of the finds. The objects acquired by The Jewish Museum, which all bear a number that begins "JM 12-73," came primarily from Tell Ajjul, Tell ed-Duweir (Lachish), and Tell Farah South, and date mostly from the Middle Bronze and Iron Ages. The material from Lachish, which forms the core of the first section of this exhibition, was excavated and given to Mr. Colt in 1932/33, and was acquired by New York University in 1940. In 1979, the ancient glass holdings were considerably augmented by a gift from Elaine and Harvey Rothenberg and again in 1981 through a donation of the Judith Riklis collection. Finally, in 1981 the major donation of the Betty and Max Ratner Collection of antiquities from Israel added immeasurably to the diversity of The Jewish Museum Collection, extending its range into the Hellenistic and Early Roman Periods. The unusual chronological range and fine quality of these objects, combined with the continuing public interest in biblical archaeology, were the sources of inspiration for the current exhibition.

Archaeology, Culture and History

by Eric Meyers

Recent years have witnessed a growing controversy over the definition of the field of biblical archaeology. At the core of this controversy is the traditional influence of biblical history and theology on the goals and field methods of archaeologists working in Israel and surrounding areas. This influence has led biblical archaeologists to concentrate primarily on texts and artifacts of those cultures related to the events described in the Bible from the time of the Patriarchs to Herod Antipas. This concentration, to a certain extent, has been in conflict with the historical development and growth of the larger field of archaeology.

Following the "collection-mania" of Victorian Europe, a heightened awareness arose in the 1920s and 1930s of the need for careful excavation and study of artifacts from the distant past. This led to the development of pottery seriation studies that linked changes in pottery style to chronology, and the refinement of the grid system of excavation in order to better understand and record the original context of artifacts. Although the 1940s and 1950s continued the trend toward a more systematic analysis of data, it was also a period in which many still believed that biblical archaeology's primary goal was the corroboration of Scripture. The most famous publication that espoused this point of view was Werner Keller's *The Bible as History*, an incorrect translation of the German title, which would be more correctly rendered as "The Bible is Indeed Correct." At the same time, the archaeologist and biblical scholar Nelson Glueck began to explore Israel and Jordan, using the Bible as his guide in associating ancient events with archaeological remains. This mixing of archaeology, theology and history is the unique legacy and chief characteristic of biblical archaeology.

In the 1960s the so-called new archaeology, which had originated in the 1950s, finally began to make its mark on biblical archaeologists. Emerging from the American tradition of anthropological archaeology, it introduced an environmental focus, a concern for socio-cultural approaches, and a reliance on methods developed in the natural sciences for information retrieval and interpretation. Many leading archaeologists working in Israel became concerned about being identified with scientific objectivity and argued for a nomenclature that was neutral with respect to the Bible. They suggested that those engaged in archaeological work in the Holy Land and surrounding areas be known as "Palestinian archaeologists" or "Syro-Palestinian archaeologists." The change in nomenclature, they believed, would convey in a simple yet dramatic way the contemporary state of the field, and separate it from the days of the not so distant past when giants like W. F. Albright, Nelson Glueck, and Father de Vaux were preoccupied with correlating the biblical record with archaeological evidence. Even traditional biblical archaeologists like G. Ernest Wright, President of the American Schools of Oriental Research during the 1960s and Albright's leading disciple in field archaeology, felt that the seeds of change had been sown.

Biblical archaeology, as conducted by Americans at least, was never to be the same again. For example, many previously untapped sources of information and archaeological sub-specialties now became regular components of the broad discipline of archaeology. The bones, both human and animal, which previous generations had discarded, were now cleaned and boxed and sent to specialists all over the world for examination. The same earth that late nineteenth- and early twentieth-century archaeologists had viewed as an expendable and annoying blanket covering hidden artifacts was now sifted and screened for minute seeds and tiny artifacts. Geologists who were once concerned only with the depositional history of a site were now conducting research on the provenance of specific stones, metals, and clays used in artifacts, and commenting on the region as a whole and the resources it provided for city and village life. Physical scientists and biological scientists alike were now engaged in a dialogue about ancient ecology.

The greatest impact on biblical archaeology in the 1970s was the concern of social scientists for the reconstruction of social patterns. The examination of the history of the human community, when carried out in the light of the broader cultural perspective of anthropology and combined with more meticulous field techniques, enabled historians and some traditional biblical archaeologists to begin to ask an entirely new set of questions about ancient life. Those scholars might otherwise have embarked upon a far narrower investigation were they to have approached a given cultural epoch or group from the perspective of literary history alone. Thus, one's place in the debate about the definition of biblical archaeology is determined more by what one brings to the field by way of training, background, and theoretical considerations (i.e., anthropology, philology, or history) than by what one brings out of the ground.

Although biblical archaeology has grown and developed during the past few decades, some of the old pitfalls are still very much with us. Expeditions still set out to identify places, events, and objects that are identified only in historical or, more precisely, biblical terms. An example would be an expedition whose goal is the recovery of Noah's wooden Ark. Even if a wooden ark were found (which would be preserved only under the most unusual circumstances), and even if it were dated to the right period, it would be almost impossible to identify it as that specific ark

without inscriptional evidence.

The influence of biblical studies on biblical archaeology has had an impact on a variety of levels, ranging from large-scale cultural reconstructions to the interpretation of individual artifacts unearthed during excavations. Although the Bible is an important source of information, it can only be used secondarily by the archaeologist to interpret his finds. The primary means of interpretation must remain an analysis of the context within which the objects were found and, if it can be reconstructed, the cultural context within which they were used.

A recent example of the re-evaluation of artifacts based primarily on archaeological context is the interpretation of the large "standing stones" found on many sites from the Bronze Age through the Iron Age. Traditionally, these large, column-like slabs of stone have been connected to the *massebot* mentioned in the Bible. *Massebot* are free-standing stones used for religious ceremonies, as when Jacob set up a pillar to mark his experience at Bethel (Gen. 28:18). While it is undoubtedly true that many of the stones found in excavations, especially those found close to areas containing altars and cultic vessels, are indeed *massebot*, one archaeologist has recently observed that many are really structural pillars used to support the roof of buildings. This interpretation is based on archaeological context and fits in with the widespread evidence for rows of columns in the ordinary domestic "four-room" house of the Iron Age.

The history of the interpretation of Level III at Lachish also highlights both the influence of the Bible on archaeological research and the importance of relying primarily on internal evidence before correlating archaeological data with historical events.

The ancient Judean city of Lachish was an important administrative center during the period of the Divided Kingdom (928–586 BCE).

According to the Book of Kings, Lachish was one of the settlements razed to the ground by the Assyrian king Sennacherib at the end of the eighth century BCE. This event is also recorded in the annals of Sennacherib and depicted on a wall relief at the king's palace at Nineveh.

Beginning with the British expedition to Lachish in the 1930s, archaeologists have tried to identify the destruction level that is to be attributed to the Assyrians. The British found two levels (III and II) that were covered by thick layers of rubble and debris, probable remnants from the massive destruction of Lachish at two different times.

Level II, the uppermost level, was recognized as the city destroyed by the Babylonians in 586 BCE, primarily because it was the uppermost level, and was followed by a period of partial abandonment, a situation one might expect during the period of the Exile. In addition, Level II also yielded the Lachish Letters, correspondences of inscribed pot sherds to and from the commander of the Lachish garrison to surrounding settlements. The correspondence describes a panicked situation immediately preceding the invasion by, presumably, the Babylonians, even referring to the warnings of a "prophet." Based on the historical situation depicted and the orthography of the script, it seems fairly certain that the letters are to be dated to the time immediately preceding the conquest of Judah by the Babylonians.

The seven-foot-thick debris that covered the Level III city could then be attributed to either the first Babylonian campaign in 597 BCE or to the Assyrians in 701 BCE. The archaeologists analyzed the problem first on the basis of internal evidence. The director of the British expedition compared the pottery forms from Levels III and II to discern how much change in form had taken place between the two levels. He concluded that the pottery from the two levels was almost identical and that therefore only a short period had elapsed; this led him to believe that Level III was destroyed in 597 BCE.

His field assistant, who was responsible for publishing a description of the pottery some twenty years later, offered a different interpretation. She concluded that the changes in pottery forms was significant enough to warrant a hundred years difference between the levels, thus ascribing the destruction of Level III to the Assyrians in 701 BCE. The controversy was unresolved when the Tel Aviv University expedition renewed research at Lachish in the 1970s. Because of the unusual opportunity to correlate the results of archaeological and historical data, the expedition made the clarification of Level III a priority. They tested the stratigraphy from Level II down to Level VI (the latest Canaanite level) in order to see if a third destruction from the Iron Age would be revealed. If so, then the bottommost could possibly be assigned to the 701 date with the middle level attributed to 597 BCE. (Assuming, of course, that each of the destruction levels was the result of a historically documented invasion and not of natural causes or civil war.) However, in all seven areas there was no evidence for a large city being destroyed by fire—other than Level III—that could be dated to the eighth century BCE.

Further evidence from Level III also pointed to its destruction at the hands of an invading army. Hundreds of arrowheads were found close to the destroyed city wall and, as had long been predicted, the remnant of a siege ramp probably used by the Assyrians identified outside the walls of the Level III city. Using the archaeological evidence from Lachish and correlating it with the historical records, the excavators concluded that Level III was the city besieged by Sennacherib as depicted in the Nineveh wall reliefs.

We might therefore question the methods of those biblical archaeologists who still base their research on a preconceived set of historical assumptions. Drawing on a classic example from biblical studies, archaeologists relying primarily on the Bible might tend to view the beginnings of Israel in terms of a military conquest by a united group of invading troops led first by Moses and then by Joshua. Thinking largely in terms of political history, such a researcher might try to set dates for the series of battles that brought about this event, attempt to pinpoint the sites of the various encounters between Israelites and indigenous Canaanites, and trace the outlines of the ensuing Israelite tribal organization. Furthermore, he would note the destruction layers widespread on tells (mounds) in Palestine at the end of the Late Bronze Age and attribute these destructions to Joshua's might. The essential historicity of the biblical narrative would thus be corroborated, and the conception of the Israelites acquiring Canaan through a military invasion from without would be established. In such instances, the archaeological data becomes secondary to a historical situation which has a prior place in the excavator's mind before the first spade is placed into the ground.

Today, the more scientifically objective approach must analyze the archaeological results apart from biblical references. True, life in Canaan was severely disrupted at the end of the Late Bronze Age. Yet extra-biblical texts, themselves the products of archaeological excavations, indicate that peoples other than Israelites were on the move at that time, attempting to set roots in the Levant. For example, the Philistines, one of the so-called Sea Peoples who probably had emigrated from the Aegean, had settled on the Mediterranean coast shortly after the arrival of the Israelites. And indeed, on some of the destroyed levels mentioned above are found settlements with pottery clearly descended from Aegean forms, pottery indicative, it would seem, of a Philistine presence. Further, local Canaanites were struggling to gain some autonomy, and Egyptian countermeasures against Canaanite vassal cities were no doubt carried out. It is not out of the question that internecine Canaanite warfare also led to the destruction that archaeologists had long noted. In short,

the perpetrators of the destruction of any given Canaanite city at the end of the Late Bronze Age cannot be glibly identified as Israelite soldiers. The ruins themselves offer no testimony as to the source of the destruction. Even military causes cannot be posited with surety. Natural disasters or fires caused by non-military means cannot easily be ruled out. Careful analysis of the sequences of artifactual material recovered at the latest Late Bronze Age sites, and at the earliest Iron Age settlements built on their ruins, provides the puzzling information that there is a strong continuity in many aspects of the material culture. The pottery types of the Canaanite city-states are continued not only on rebuilt cities but also in the villages started anew, villages normally associated with the Israelite conquerors. This continuity of material culture cannot be understood without allowing for some continuity of population, of people using forms and techniques handed down for generations.

Such evidence demands that the archaeologist and the historian re-evaluate the notion of a conquest by outside invaders. Present theories of historical reconstruction now posit a rather different picture, which does not preclude military activity but which also tries to take into account social factors that pertain to Israelite beginnings. Such theories offer a model whereby Canaanite material culture is found at supposed Israelite sites because many of the "Israelites" were in fact refugees who had rebelled against the feudal control of Canaanite city-states. Such a rebellious peasantry, documented to a certain extent in the somewhat earlier Amarna letters (correspondence between local Canaanite rulers and the Pharaoh in Amarna), would have joined with the Israelites of the Exodus to establish the new Israelite community. Biblical history, therefore, must be treated as a complex pattern of social organization and change, with accompanying religious development, not only a catalogue of battles, kings, and prophets.

The interpretation of the function of

artifacts, and eventually the organization of ancient cultures as a whole, is based on the careful, step-by-step accumulation of levels of information. The first step is to retrieve as much information as possible, given the limitations of time, manpower, and budget. It is not only the quantity of the material recovered, but also the documentation of the locations of objects, their association with each other and with the succession of occupation, building, and destruction levels that is crucial. New methodology has also shown that it is no longer acceptable to study a site in isolation from its regional affiliations and the environmental factors operating upon both. The analysis of the sequences of strata at one site, each consisting of a combination of environmental factors, artifactual and architectural assemblages, enables the archaeologist to establish a relative chronology for each individual site. This analysis makes each site a basic building block in the reconstruction of the social patterns of the region and eventually the entire ancient civilization.

As the data from many sites are compared and correlated, the chronology of a region will ultimately be discovered. The archaeologists can then ask and answer more sophisticated questions about the political, economic, and social interactions of the sites and the people who inhabited them.

At the point at which these questions are being asked, the archaeologist will need to integrate the results of historical study with those of his own investigations. In turn, the biblical historian will rely on the cultural data of the archaeologist to help him to elucidate textual problems and to arrive at a more comprehensive view of history.

In the 1980s the discipline of archaeology has become more specialized and complex than ever before. Concomitantly, historical and philological studies, due to the discovery of thousands of new texts and the development of new methods of analyzing language, have also become increasingly demanding. As a result, archaeologists,

historians, and philologists, while focusing on the same periods and cultures, are doing so in greater isolation than ever before. This has created the need for the sharing of information in their attempts to reconstruct ancient history and culture. To put the matter in a slightly different way, we may differentiate between those scholars who emphasize the biblical *word* as the primary corpus of evidence from which all history flows, and those who emphasize the biblical *world* in its material manifestations as the primary datum from which all interpretation of history emerges. In the case of the former, there is a concentration on ancient records and an attempt to explain and pinpoint certain historical events. In the case of the latter, there is an absolute attention to the details of material remains and an attempt to isolate and identify various stages in the development of human culture without respect to any specific historical time.

The growing complexities of biblical archaeology and history have precluded the communication of research in a form that is comprehensible to scholars and to colleagues in related fields. Most scholars of the Bible cannot be critical about a particular dig or excavation report, let alone be qualified to identify an object as Late Bronze Age II or Iron Age I. Similarly, the archaeologist cannot be expected to evaluate the subtle differences between the meanings of words used in a variety of different texts. Thus, few scholars have attempted to synthesize and few have felt comfortable in suggesting issues that should be addressed by colleagues. The task, therefore, is to share in publications the type of information that allows others to assess the data in an independent way. If an honest and understandable account of materials is presented, conveying to the specialist and the interested reader the promise and the limitations of the evidence, there will be less room for misunderstandings, and fewer incidences of the cavalier use of excavated materials. The challenge for the 1980s thus would seem to be to allow both disciplines (i.e., archaeology and biblical studies) to speak with their own distinct voices while sharing information sources and working together on meaningful interpretations. Thus, the question of whether or not there should be a biblical archaeology may become unnecessary. Archaeologists will study first the remains of material culture and second, the relation of these remains to written and pictorial histories. He or she will be a biblical archaeologist not on the basis of research proceeding from the Bible but because the period under study correlates with the times and geographical areas covered by the Bible. When both specialties, archaeology and history, are integrated in a way that makes new levels of human understanding possible, then, and only then, will biblical archaeology have come of age.

The Ratner Collection

by Arielle Kozloff

Twenty years ago, on one of his many business trips to Israel, Max Ratner was faced with the familiar problem of choosing a gift to bring home to his wife, Betty. He needed something different, something exciting, and above all, something beautiful. A work of art seemed appropriate. However, since Betty was heavily involved with modern art both in Cleveland (near their home in Shaker Heights) and in Israel, a modern work did not fit the bill of something different. Max's mind leaped to the opposite end of the time spectrum—antiquity—and, remembering Betty's affinity for glass, he hurried out and bought for her a beautiful, octagonal Roman glass flagon.

Max's present so enthralled Betty that she turned her collector's instinct to this new field. Max happily encouraged her and participated in this adventure with her as much as his schedule would allow. Little did either of them realize that one Roman glass flagon bought as a souvenir would become the foundation of a large and important collection of Israeli antiquities ranging over a period of more than 4,000 years.

What drove the Ratners to acquire the sort of objects found in their collection was not greed for the unique and historically or aesthetically important works. Objects of daily life were what interested the Ratners, objects that were used not by inaccessible kings and queens, but by "ordinary people," our own ancient counterparts. As Betty Ratner said in her foreword to the 1978 catalogue of the collection: "History—when one holds in one's hands an object made forty centuries ago—becomes more than just the record of monumental events, more than a simple recording of wars or large and noble deeds. It becomes a record of the lives of ordinary people." Cupping a clay lamp in our hands, we can imagine it still warm from the hands of a distant ancestor. With one touch, we can cross the centuries to our past, to our ancient heritage. Again in the collector's words, "We all share a similar legacy . . . these artifacts tell not just the story of one people but represent the story of the beginnings of all people."

A romantic feeling of familiarity with antiquity is really only a bonus of the Ratner collection. Its true strength lies in its comprehensiveness. From flint knife to bronze bread stamp, this collection chronicles the development of common crafts in the Holy Land from the end of the Neolithic Period (ca. 4000 BCE) to the Byzantine (fifth to sixth century CE). The evolution of ceramics progresses from an Early Bronze Age coil-built pitcher to Middle Bronze Age wheel-thrown carinated bowls to a complex Iron Age pilgrim flask made of wheel-thrown and molded parts joined together.

By far the greatest amount of the material in the Ratner collection comes from the Iron Age through the Roman Period. It is a selection of these objects that appears in the present exhibition. Small female fertility figurines and terra cotta bird figurines speak to us of a time when the Canaanites worshipped Ba'al and Astarte (Ishtar), his female counterpart. Apparently the Israelites periodically succumbed to the attraction of these cult practices for which, according to the Book of Judges, they were severely punished.

Unfortunately, there are no early Iron Age objects that can be attributed to a specifically Jewish ritual. The commercial side of Iron Age life is recorded by a stone weight and bronze currency rings. A fine example of Iron Age pottery is the "pilgrim flask," which was used to hold water or wine and may have been used by travelers.

The periods of the Babylonian Exile and the later Persian occupation are reflected in objects such as the alabaster cosmetic palette. The Persians were followed by Alexander the Great, who made Hellenism the way of life, especially in the coastal cities. Greek influence is measured in sculpture and jewelry from the sixth to the third centuries BCE. Roman tastes are reflected in a terra cotta lamp with a scene of fighting gladiators and coins with the countenances of Roman emperors.

Yet through all of these centuries of foreign occupation, Jewish integrity and practices remained intact. Preparation of grain offerings for the joyous feast of *Succot* are evoked in a basalt tripod mortar and pestle. A beautiful stone ossuary reminds us of the more solemn custom of reburying properly disintegrated human remains in stone chests in burial chambers. The Roman bronze pitcher, its handle terminating at the top with a human figure and at the bottom with a Medusa head, would have compromised Jewish law against having graven images except that the ancient owner had very carefully filed away the offending faces.

The Ratners like to jest that because they ran out of room in their home they were forced to put the collection on public view. However, it was truly their humanity, their sensitivity that drove them to share their collection. In May of 1978, the first exhibition of their collection opened at Park Synagogue in Cleveland Heights. This exhibition, THE FIRST 4000 YEARS, then traveled for three years to fifteen locations in the United States and Canada under the auspices of the Smithsonian Institution Traveling Exhibition Service.

During this tour Joy Ungerleider-Mayerson, then Director of The Jewish Museum, approached the Ratners about the possibility of donating their collection to The Jewish Museum. Because of a great demand for archaeological exhibitions at the museum, the gift was needed imminently. It is a rare collector who parts with his collection, gathered lovingly piece by piece, during his own lifetime. Yet the grace with which the Ratners immediately turned over their collection belied any pain involved.

Two thousand years ago one of the glass perfume bottles in the collection may have been presented by an affectionate husband to his lovely wife. Two decades ago the repetition of this gift made it a legacy. By the donation of their collection to The Jewish Museum, where it will become part of its permanent exhibitions, the Ratners continue the legacy, not just materially, but in the true spirit of philanthropy—a love for all people and for our common patrimony.

Bibliography

Alexander, Christine
1928   *Jewelry. The Art of the Goldsmith in Classical Times as Illustrated in the Museum Collection.* New York: Metropolitan Museum of Art.

Amiran, R.
1970   *Ancient Pottery of the Holy Land.* Rutgers University Press.

Ashdod I
1967   *Excavations at Ashdod I,* by M. Dothan and D. N. Freedman. *Atiqot* 7 (English series).

Ashdod II–III
1971   *Ashdod II-III,* by M. Dothan. *Atiqot* 9–10 (English series).

Auth, S. H.
1976   *Ancient Glass at the Newark Museum.* Newark, N.J.: Barton Press, Inc.

Avigad, Nahman
1962   "The Expedition to the Judean Desert, 1961: Expedition A," *Israel Exploration Journal* 12: 169–83.
1970   "Excavations in the Jewish Quarter of the Old City of Jerusalem, 1969/70," *Israel Exploration Journal* 20: 1–8, 129–40.
1972   "Excavations in the Jewish Quarter of the Old City of Jerusalem, 1971," *Israel Exploration Journal* 22: 193–200.
1976   *Archaeological Discoveries in the Jewish Quarter of Jerusalem—Second Temple Period.* Jerusalem: Israel Exploration Society and the Israel Museum.
1977   *Beth Shearim* v. III (Hebrew). Jerusalem: Masada Press.
1980   *The Upper City of Jerusalem* (Hebrew). Jerusalem: Shiqmonah.

Bailey, D. M.
1980   *A Catalogue of the Lamps in the British Museum* v. 2: *Roman Lamps Made in Italy.* London.

Bar Adon, Pesach
1977   "Another Settlement of the Judean Desert Sect at 'En el-Ghuweir on the Shores of the Dead Sea," *Bulletin of the American Schools of Oriental Research* 227: 1–25.

Barag, Dan
1962   "Glass Vessels from the Cave of Horror," *Israel Exploration Journal* 12: 208–14.
1966   "The Glass Aryballos," *Atiqot* 5 (English series): 58–9.
1970   "Glass Pilgrim Vessels from Jerusalem, Part I," *Journal of Glass Studies* 12: 35–54.
1971a   "The Glass Vessels," *Atiqot* 9–10 (English series): 202–5.
1971b   "Glass Pilgrim Vessels from Jerusalem, Parts II and III," *Journal of Glass Studies* 13: 45–63.
1972   "Two Roman Glass Bottles with Remnants of Oil," *Israel Exploration Journal* 22: 24–27.

Basch, A.
1972   "Analysis of Oil from Two Roman Glass Bottles," *Israel Exploration Journal* 22: 27–32.

Baur, Paul C.
1922   *Catalogue of the Rebecca Darlington Stoddard Collection of Greek and Italian Vases in Yale University.* New Haven: Yale University Press.

Berger, Paul-Richard
1973   *Die neubabylonischen Königinschriften.* Kevelaer: Butzon & Bercker.

Beth Shan III
1931   *Beth-Shan III: Excavations 1921–23, The Arab and Byzantine Levels,* by G. M. Fitzgerald. Philadelphia: The University Museum, University of Pennsylvania.

Beth Shan
1966   *The Iron Age at Beth-Shan,* by Frances W. James. Philadelphia: The University Museum, University of Pennsylvania.

Bethany
1957   *Excavations at Bethany,* by Fr. S. J. Saller. Jerusalem: Franciscan Press.

Brilliant, Richard
1979   *Pompeii 79 AD.* New York: Clarkson N. Potter, Inc.

Callendar, M. H.
1965   *Roman Amphorae.* London: Oxford University Press.

Casson, Lionel
1981   "Maritime Trade in Antiquity," *Archaeology* 34: 37–43.

Charlesworth, Dorothy
1966   "Roman Square Bottles," *Journal of Glass Studies* 8: 26–40.

Corinth
1930   *Corinth v. IV, pt. II: Terracotta Lamps,* by Oscar Broneer. Cambridge: Harvard University Press.

Crowfoot, J. W., and G. M. Fitzgerald
1927   *Excavations in the Tyropoeon Valley, Jerusalem.* Palestine Exploration Fund Annual.

Culican, W.
1973   "Phoenician Jewellery in New York and Copenhagen," *Berytus* 22: 31–52.

Dayton, J.
1974   "Money in the Near East before Coinage," *Berytus* 23: 41–52.

de Franciscis, A.
1962   "Vetri antichi scoperti ad Ercolano," *Journal of Glass Studies* 5: 137–39.

Deneauve, Jean
1969   *Lampes de Carthage.* Paris: Editions du Centre National de la Recherche Scientifique.

de Vaux, Roland
1954   "Fouilles au Khirbet Qumrân: Rapport Préliminaire sur la deuxième Campagne," *Revue Biblique* 61: 206–36.
1959   "Fouilles de Feshkha, Rapport Préliminaire, *Revue Biblique* 66: 225–55.
1961   *Ancient Israel: Its Life and Institutions.* New York: McGraw Hill.

Diban
1972   "The Excavations at Dibon (Dhiban) in Moab," by A. D. Tushingham. *Annual of the American Schools of Oriental Research* v. 40.

Diehl
1927   *Inscriptiones Latinae Christianae Veteres II.* Berlin.

Diringer, David
1941   "On Ancient Hebrew Inscriptions Discovered at Tell ed-Duweir (Lachish) I," *Palestine Exploration Quarterly* 1941: 38–109.

Dusenberry, E.
1967   "Ancient Glass from the Cemetery of Samothrace," *Journal of Glass Studies* 9: 34–49.

Duval, N.
(n.d.)   *La Mosaique Funeraire dans l'Art Paleochrétien.* Ravenna: Longo.

Fortuna, M. T.
1965   "I Vetri Soffiati della Necropoli di Akko," *Journal of Glass Studies,* 7: 17–25.

Frey, P. Jean-Baptiste
1975   *Corpus of Jewish Inscriptions.* New York: Ktav Publishing House, Inc.

Garrucci, Raffaele
1865   *Dissertazioni archeologiche di vario argomento.* Roma II.

Gezer II
1967-70 *Report of the 1967–70 Seasons in Fields I and II,* by W. G. Dever, et al. Jerusalem: Hebrew Union College/Nelson Glueck School of Biblical Archaeology.

Goodenough, Erwin R.
1953   *Jewish Symbols in the Greco-Roman Period* v. III. New York: Pantheon Books.

Greifenhagen, A.
1970 *Schmuckarbeiter in Eden Metall*, v. I. Staatliche Museen zu Berlin. Berlin: Mann.

Grose, D.
1977 "Early Blown Glass," *Journal of Glass Studies* 19: 9–29.

Gutmann, Joseph
1964 *Jewish Ceremonial Art*. New York: Thomas Yoseloff.

Hachlili, Rachel
1980 "A Second Temple Period Jewish Necropolis in Jericho," *Biblical Archaeologist* 43: 235–40.

Hak, S.
1965 "Contribution d'une découvert archaeologique récent a l'étude du la verrerie Syrienne à l'epoque Romaine," *Journal of Glass Studies* 7: 26–34.

Harden, Donald B.
1969 "Ancient Glass II: Roman," *Archaeological Journal* 126: 44–77.

Harding, L.
1951 "A Roman Tomb in Amman," *Annual of the Department of Antiquities of Jordan* I: 34–36.

Hayes, J. W.
1975 *Roman and Pre-Roman Glass in the Royal Ontario Museum*. Toronto: Royal Ontario Museum.

Hendin, David
1976 *Guide to Ancient Jewish Coins*. New York: Attic Books Ltd.

Hennessy, J. B.
1970 "Excavations at Samaria-Sebaste, 1968," *Levant* 2: 1–21.

Hestrin, Ruth and Michal Dayagi-Mendels
1979 *Inscribed Seals*. Jerusalem: Israel Museum.

Higgins, R.
1961 *Greek and Roman Jewelry*. London: Methuen and Co., Ltd.

Hoffman, H. and P. Davidson
1966 *Greek Gold*. Boston: Museum of Fine Arts; Brooklyn: Brooklyn Museum; Richmond: Virginia Museum of Fine Arts.

Holland, T. A.
1977 "A Study of Palestinian Iron Age Baked Clay Figurines, with Special Reference to Jerusalem: Cave 1," *Levant* 9: 121–55.

Iliffe, J. H.
1944 "Imperial Art in Trans-Jordan, Figurines and Lamps from a Potter's Store at Jerash," *Quarterly of the Department of Antiquities of Palestine* 11, nos. 1–2: 1–26.

Jeremias, Joachim
1969 *Jerusalem in the Time of Jesus*. Philadelphia: Fortress.

Josephus, Flavius
1959 *The Jewish War*, translated by G. A. Williamson. Baltimore: Penguin Books.

Kahane, P. P.
1961 "Rock Cut Tombs at Huqoq. Notes on the Finds," *Atiqot* 3 (English series): 126–47.

Kande, N. Y.
(n. d.) Sale Catalogue no. 78.

Kozloff, Arielle
1978 *The First 4000 Years; The Ratner Collection of Judean Antiquities*. Cleveland, Ohio: Park Synagogue.

Lachish II
1940 *Lachish II*, by O. Tufnell, C. Inge, and L. Harding. London: Oxford University Press.

Lachish III
1953 *Lachish III*, by O. Tufnell. London: Oxford University Press.

Lachish V
1975 *Lachish V*, by Y. Aharoni. Tel Aviv: Gateway Publishers Inc.

Lapp, Nancy (ed.)
1964 "The Third Campaign at Tell el-Fûl; the Excavations of 1964," *Annual of the American Schools of Oriental Research* v. 45.

Lapp, Paul
1961 *Palestinian Ceramic Chronology 200 BC–AD 70*. New Haven: American Schools of Oriental Research.

Lapp, Paul (ed.)
1968 *The 1957 Excavations at Beth-Zur. Annual of the American Schools of Oriental Research*, v. 38.

Lapp, P., and N. Lapp
1958 "A Comparative Study of a Hellenistic Pottery Group from Beth-Zur," *Bulletin of the American Schools of Oriental Research* v. 151: 16–27.

Lapp, Paul, and N. Lapp (eds.)
1974 *Discoveries in the Wadi Ed-Dâliyeh. Annual of the American Schools of Oriental Research* v. 41.

Lemaire, A.
1980 "A Note on Inscription XXX from Lachish," *Tel Aviv* 7: 92–94.

Leon, Harry J.
1960 *The Jews of Ancient Rome*. Philadelphia: Jewish Publication Society of America.

Levi, Peter
1980 *Atlas of the Greek World*. New York: Facts on File, Inc.

Masada
1966 *Masada*, by Y. Yadin. New York: Random House.

Matheson, S. B.
1980 *Ancient Glass in the Yale University Art Gallery*. Meriden, Ct.: The Meriden Gravure Company, Yale University Printing Service.

Mattlingly, H.
1940 *Coins of the Roman Empire*, v. IV. London: British Museum Catalogue.

Mau, August
1899 *Pompeii, Its Life and Art*. Translated by F. W. Kelsey. New York: The Macmillan Company.

Mazar, Benjamin
1969 *The Excavations in the Old City of Jerusalem*. Jerusalem: Israel Exploration Society.
1971 *The Excavations in the Old City of Jerusalem Near the Temple Mount*. Jerusalem: The Institute of Archeology, Hebrew University, The Israel Exploration Society.

Mazar, B., and T. Dothan
1966 *Ein Gedi, the First and Second Seasons of Excavations 1961–62. Atiqot* V (English series).

McClees, Helen
1941 *The Daily Life of the Greeks and Romans*. New York: Metropolitan Museum of Art.

Megiddo Tombs
1938 *Megiddo Tombs*, by P. L. O. Guy. Oriental Institute Publications 33. Chicago: University of Chicago.

Megiddo I
1939 *Megiddo I. Seasons of 1925–34*, by R. Lamon and G. Shipton. Oriental Institute Publications 42. Chicago: University of Chicago.

Megiddo II
1948 *Megiddo II. Seasons of 1935–39*, by G. Loud. Oriental Institute Publications 62. Chicago: University of Chicago.

Megiddo Cult
1935 *Material Remains of the Megiddo Cult*, by H. G. May. Oriental Institute Publications 26. Chicago: University of Chicago Press.

Menzel, Heinz
1954 *Antike Lampen im Römische-Germanischen Zentralmuseum zu Mainz*. Katalog 15. Mainz: Verlag des Römisch-Germanischen Zentralmuseums.

Meshorer, Ya'akov
1967   *Jewish Coins of the Second Temple Period.* Translated by I. H. Levine. Tel Aviv: Am Hassefer.
1978   "Early Means of Payment and the First Coinage," *Ariel* 45–46: 127–43.
forthcoming
    Coins Reveal. New York: The Jewish Museum.

Meyers, Carol
1976   *The Tabernacle Menorah.* Missoula: American Schools of Oriental Research.

Meyers, Carol, and Eric Meyers
1975   "Another Jewish Bread Stamp," *Israel Exploration Journal* 25: 154–55.

Meyers, Eric
1971   *Jewish Ossuaries: Reburial and Rebirth. Biblica et Orientalia* 24.

Nachtergael, G.
1978   *La Collection Marcel Hombert.* Brussels: Papyrologica Bruxellensia 15.

Negbi, Ora
1966   "A Deposit of Terracottas and Statuettes from Tel Sippor," *Atiqot* 6 (English series): 1–22.

Negev, Avraham
1980   *Archaeological Encyclopedia of the Holy Land.* Englewood: SBS Publisher.

Nessena
1962   *Excavations at Nessena*, vols. I–II, ed. by H. Dunscombe Colt. London: British School of Archaeology in Jerusalem.

Netzer, E., and Eric Meyers
1977   "Preliminary Report on the Joint Jericho Excavation Project," *Bulletin of the American Schools of Oriental Research* 228: 15–27.

Oliver, Andrew, Jr.
1977   *Silver for the Gods.* Toledo, Ohio: The Toledo Museum of Art.

Overbeck, J.
1856   *Pompeji.* Leipzig: Verlag von Wilhelm Engelmann.

Paul, Shalom, and William Dever
1974   *Biblical Archaeology.* New York: Quadrangle/The New York Times Book Co.

Radan, G.
1961   "A Greek Helmet Discovered off the Coast of Turkey," *Israel Exploration Journal* 11: 176–80.

Rahmani, L. Y.
1980   "A Jewish Rock-cut Tomb on Mt. Scopus," *Atiqot* 14 (English series): 49–54.

Reifenberg, A.
1936   "Jüdische Lampen," *Journal of the Palestine Oriental Society* 16: 166–77.
1939   "Ancient Jewish Stamps," *Palestine Exploration Quarterly* 1939: 193–98.

Richter, Gisela M. A.
1915   *Greek, Etruscan and Roman Bronzes.* New York: Metropolitan Museum of Art.

Rowe, A.
1940   *The Four Canaanite Temples of Beth Shan*, Part I. Philadelphia: University of Pennsylvania, University Museum Press.

Samaria-Sebaste III
1957   *Samaria-Sebaste III: The Objects*, by J. Crowfoot, G. Crowfoot and A. Kenyon. London: Palestine Exploration Fund.

Sams, G. Kenneth
1977   "Beer in the City of Midas," *Archaeology* 30: 108–15.

Schoder, Raymond, S. J.
(n. d.)   *Masterpieces of Greek Art.* Connecticut: New York Geographic Society.

Shiloh, Yigal
1970   "The Four-Room House. Its Situation and Function in the Israelite City," *Israel Exploration Journal* 20: 180–88.
1978   "Elements in the Development of Town Planning in the Israelite City," *Israel Exploration Journal* 28: 36–51.
1979   "Iron Age Sanctuaries and Cult Elements in Palestine," *Symposia*, ed. by Frank Moore Cross, pp. 147–58. Cambridge: American Schools of Oriental Research.
1980   "Jerusalem: The City of David," *Archaeology* 33: 8–17.

Smith, R. H.
1964   "The Household Lamp of Palestine in Old Testament Times," *Biblical Archaeologist* 27, no. 1: 2–31.

Sussman, Varda
1970   *Jewish Art on Lamps in the Time of the Mishna.* Jerusalem: The Israel Museum.
1972   *Ornamented Jewish Oil Lamps: From the Fall of the Second Temple through the Revolt of Bar Kocheba* (Hebrew). Jerusalem: The Bialik Institute and the Israel Exploration Society.

Swedish Cyprus Expedition
1948   *Swedish Cyprus Expedition* IV, pt. 2, by Einar Gjerstad. Stockholm: Victor Petterson Bokindustrjaktiebolag.

Tadmor, Miriam and Osnat Misch-Brandl
1980   "The Beth Shemesh Hoard of Jewellery," *The Israel Museum News* 16: 71–82.

Thompson, Homer
1934   "Two Centuries of Hellenistic Pottery," *Hesperia* 3: 311–480.

Tsori, Nehemiah
1977   "Roman Stamped Amphora Handles from Beth-Shean" *Israel Exploration Journal* 27: 125–6.

Ussishkin, David
1976   "Royal Judean Storage Jars and Private Seal Impressions," *Bulletin of the American Schools of Oriental Research* 223: 1–13.
1977   "The Destruction of Lachish by Sennacherib and the Dating of the Royal Judean Storage Jars," *Tel Aviv* 4: 28–60.
1978   "Excavations at Tel Lachish, 1973–1977, Preliminary Report," *Tel Aviv* 5, nos. 1–2.

Vogelstein and Rieger
1896   *Geschichte der Juden in Rom*, Leipzig.

Wegner, M.
1939   *Die Herrscherbildnisse in antoninischer Zeit.* Berlin.

Weinberg, Gladys
1970   "Hellenistic Glass from Tel Anafa in Upper Galilee," *Journal of Glass Studies* 12: 17–27.

Weinberg, Saul
1969   "Tel Anafa—A Problem-Oriented Excavation," *Muse* 3: 16–23.

Welten, P.
1969   *Die Königs-Stempel.* Wiesbaden: Harrassowitz.

Wright, G. R. H.
1971   "Pre-Israelite Temples in the Land of Canaan," *Palestine Exploration Quarterly* 103: 17–32.

Yadin, Yigal
1961   "The Expedition to the Judean Desert, 1960: Expedition D," *Israel Exploration Journal* 11: 36–52.
1965   "The Excavations of Masada 1963/64," *Israel Exploration Journal* 15, nos. 1–2.
1975   *Hazor.* New York: Random House.

Yale Oriental Series IX
1937   *Votive and Historical Texts from Babylonia and Assyria*, by F. Stephens, pp. 36–37.

Zemer, Avshalom
1978   *Storage Jars in Ancient Sea Trade*, second edition. Haifa: National Maritime Museum Foundation.

Zevulun, Uza and Yael Olenik
1979   *Function and Design in the Talmudic Period*, second edition. Tel Aviv: Haaretz Museum.

Notes to the Catalogue

The first line in each entry, after the title, denotes the place
where the object was produced (its origin). In the
case of excavated objects, this line states the name of the site and
the find spot. When a piece does not have an excavated origin,
the area to which its origin is attributed stylistically appears on
the first line. Any information on the piece's last known
provenance has been placed on the line before the credit line.

The second line of each entry denotes the archaeological period
in which the object was made, followed by the date. This date
indicates a time range for the production of the object within the
larger archaeological period; it is not necessarily equivalent to the
dates for the entire period. The chronology of dates for archaeological
periods followed in this catalogue was taken from the *Encyclopedia of
Archaeological Excavations in the Holy Land,* (English edition), edited
by Michael Avi-Yonah and Ephraim Stern, Massada Press, Jerusalem,
1978. In the case of objects which were produced outside of Israel,
we have adopted the names for the archaeological periods used
in the countries of origin. Thus, one will see the use of the term
Late Hellenistic for objects originating somewhere in the
eastern Mediterranean in the 2nd to 1st centuries BCE, and the term
Hasmonean for objects made in Israel during the same period.

The letters "BCE" after a date stand for "Before the Common
Era"; the letters "CE" stand for "Common Era."

All measurements were taken at the points of maximum dimension.

The year that a particular purchase or gift was
made, if known, has been placed at the end of the provenance or credit
line. The accession numbers of pieces obtained from 1979
onward begin with the year of acquisition.

Abbreviations, spellings of names and transliterations
are based on the *Encyclopedia Judaica,* 1971 edition. All biblical
quotations were taken from the Jewish Publication Society Bible.

Clockwise from jug: no.
42; no. 37; no. 59;
necklace, no. 48; no. 39; no. 38.

Aspects of Religion, the Home, and the State

Introduction: Biblical History and the Archaeology of Lachish

During the first 200 years of the Iron Age (1200–1000 BCE), Canaan underwent a series of historical and cultural changes that would drastically alter the political and social life of the region for the next 500 years. In historical terms, this period began with the entry of the Hebrew tribes into Canaan and, some fifty years later, the arrival and settlement of the Philistines on the Mediterranean coast. After a century of bitter rivalry for political control, the Israelite tribes united under David to subdue the Philistines and establish a monarchic empire: for the first time in its history, one local government controlled Canaan.

For the archaeologist, however, such historical events are generally anonymous. In the archaeological record, invasions may be translated into destruction levels and prosperity into building levels, but the identity of the invaders or the builders usually cannot be discerned on the basis of archaeological evidence alone. Thus, the archaeologist defines history on the basis of changes in material culture over time, and not a priori on political events known from historical sources.

In archaeological terms, the period from 1200 to 586 BCE is the Iron Age, deriving its name from the first widespread use of iron tools, weapons, and jewelry. It is further subdivided into three shorter periods (see figure 1), each of which is distinguished by gradual stylistic changes in items of material culture such as pottery, by changes in settlement patterns including the large-scale abandonment or destruction of sites, and/or by changes in technology, such as the spread of the use of iron.

The Judean city of Lachish is an example par excellence of an Iron Age site in Israel. Excavations have revealed a series of destructions and rebuildings that reflect the various fortunes of Israel and Judah, ranging from periods of great prosperity to invasion and conquest by foreign armies. For the most part, the checkered history of Lachish is paralleled by the archaeological record of other cities throughout the region. For this reason, Lachish has been selected for this exhibition as a type site for the Iron Age, where one may trace both material cultural transformations through archaeology and the historical flow of events.

Lachish is an enormous tell (mound), composed of many super-imposed layers each containing the remains of one specific cultural phase in the history of the city. It is situated in a mountain pass in the Judean hills southwest of Jerusalem (see map). It was first excavated in the 1930s by the Wellcome-Marston expedition, whose work was halted prematurely by the death of its chief archaeologist. However, excavations had proceeded far enough for one of the field assistants to publish a detailed account of their finds from the Persian Period (586–330 BCE), the Iron Age, and the Bronze Ages.

The great mound then lay untouched for almost thirty years until 1966, when Yohanan Aharoni of Tel Aviv University mounted a small excavation to explore and re-examine the Persian Period temple first discovered by the Wellcome-Marston expedition. The intriguing results of Aharoni's excavations, especially his finding of an Iron Age "cult room," encouraged Tel Aviv University to plan a much larger operation to clarify several archaeological and historical problems of the Iron Age. Thus, in 1973, renewed, large-scale excavations began under the leadership of David Ussishkin. The results of these three expeditions have enabled the following reconstruction of the sequence of cultures and their fates.

The massive Late Bronze Age city of Lachish came to a dramatic end in about 1200 BCE. It was one of many thriving Canaanite urban centers that were reduced to rubble and left uninhabited or, at best, partially resettled during the twelfth and eleventh centuries BCE. It is uncertain whether the destruction of Lachish and other cities can be attributed to the invading Israelite tribes; on archaeological grounds, it is possible that the city was razed to the ground by the Philistines or Egyptians or was destroyed by natural causes, such as fire.

By the time that David established the Israelite state (at the beginning of Iron II A, ca. 1000 BCE), Lachish had begun to be resettled (Level V), although it is unclear to what extent the city was repopulated and rebuilt. The first phase of its revitalization is marked by the construction of a large edifice, interpreted as a "palace fort," on the highest point of the tell directly over the remains of temples from the preceding Bronze Age. This disregard for the sanctity of a temple site seems to indicate a cultural break with the traditions of the previous Canaanite people who had used that locale for temple construction since the third millennium. Similar conversions of sacred areas of the Bronze Age to secular spaces by the inhabitants of Iron Age levels were also noted by the excavators of Hazor and Megiddo. While this might be taken as sound archaeological evidence of the arrival and entrenchment of a totally new group of people, many aspects of material culture (e.g., pottery forms) continued from Bronze Age Canaanite levels into Iron Age levels. This combination of continuity and change is a paradox that characterizes much of the archaeological record of Iron Age Israel; it is perhaps an indication that a local culture assimilated with a new people or that well-entrenched local customs were adopted by a newly-settled group.

Lachish, unlike contemporary Iron Age cities such as Megiddo and Hazor, was not one of the settlements thoroughly fortified during the building campaigns of Solomon. Rather, it was only after the division of the kingdom (ca. 928 BCE) that Lachish (Levels IV and III) flourished and, as is shown by the growing number of private homes, increased in population. In the center of the city, the "palace-fort" of the preceding period was partially rebuilt and enlarged, becoming the single largest edifice of the Iron Age so far excavated in Israel. The city was also fortified with two walls that ringed the whole settlement, allowing entrance only through a monumental city gate. The "palace-fort" may have been constructed as part of these new Iron Age defenses, or, based on its imposing size and location on the highest point of the tell, perhaps as the administrative center or the residence of a city or regional governor.

Level III was brought to an end by a massive destruction, which left a layer of ash and rubble up to seven feet thick. Historical sources tell us that at the end of the eighth century BCE, Israel and Judah came increasingly under the shadow of the Assyrian empire to the east. By the last two decades of the century, the Assyrian armies repeatedly campaigned in the Levant, conquering most of the region and deporting the population of the Northern Kingdom of Israel (the so-called ten lost tribes). These events are recorded in the Bible and the Assyrian annals of Sennacherib. They are also depicted on the famous wall reliefs found in the Assyrian king's capital at Nineveh, which show the Assyrians besieging Lachish using a ramp and battering rams, and the marching away of the defeated Judeans. The fortifications depicted on the reliefs are almost identical to those found in Level III of the city. Thus, both the archaeological and textual evidence seem to indicate that Level III was destroyed by the Assyrians, providing an all too rare confluence of historical and archaeological data.

The succeeding settlement (Level II) was rebuilt on a smaller scale than Level III, without the large "palace-fort" that had dominated the mound since the mid-tenth century BCE. Despite this disruption on the administrative level, the material culture (especially the pottery) continued relatively unchanged. This seems to indicate a continuation of the local population in a city that decreased in its regional importance.

The Level II city suffered the same fate as its predecessor, massive and whole-scale destruction. It is generally agreed, based on archaeological and historical sources, that this destruction is to be attributed to the Babylonians, for the level above (from the Persian Period) is poorly settled as one might expect of the period following the depopulation of the region. Thus ends the Iron Age and begins a new era in the history of Israel: The Exile.

Archaeology and the Religion of the Iron Age (Nos. 1–13)

In its broadest sense religion may be defined as a set of shared beliefs and ideas that are expressed through special individual and communal behavior. Generally, an understanding of the *beliefs* and *ideas* of ancient Israelite religion lies beyond the scope of archaeological research. As a science that studies material culture as its primary data, archaeology usually can only shed light on religious *behavior* as manifested in objects and structures. This is especially so for ancient Israel, where pictorial representations are almost non-existent and where writings that describe the beliefs behind the manufacture of specially-made artifacts or the construction of a holy place are rare. Ultimately, our understanding of ancient Israelite beliefs must rest on the Bible, which is first and foremost a statement of religious faith and is beyond the corroboration of archaeology and history.

For Iron Age Israel, the limitations of archaeology are exacerbated by its inability to reveal direct evidence about the physical and spiritual center of ancient Judaism: the Temple built by Solomon in Jerusalem. It is doubtful that remains of the Temple survived the Babylonian conquest of Jerusalem in 586 BCE or the thorough reshaping of the area during Herodian times (first century BCE).

Unable to study the remains of the original Temple, archaeologists have had to look

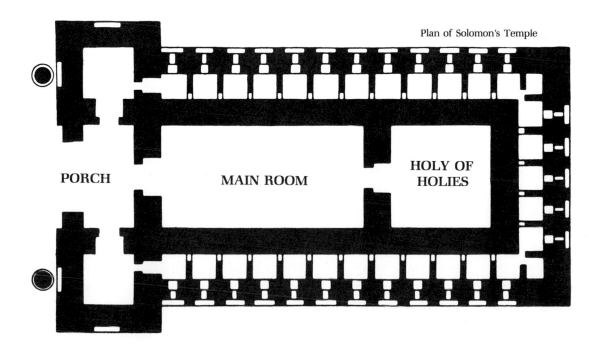

Plan of Solomon's Temple

PORCH   MAIN ROOM   HOLY OF HOLIES

elsewhere to illumine the biblical description of the Temple plan (see illustration, p. 31). They originally sought parallels in Egypt and Mesopotamia, whose well-known temples seemed to offer the most likely inspiration for the ancient Israelites. However, it was in Syria (Tainat, Alalakh) and then in Israel itself (Hazor, Arad) that archaeologists have unearthed structures whose layout and architectural elements are reminiscent of the biblical descriptions of Solomon's Temple. Although no site has yet offered a plan that exactly matches the biblical blueprint, the similarities do indicate that the origin of the plan of the Jerusalem Temple should be sought in traditions developed in Canaan.

These comparisons have enhanced our understanding of the form of the Temple. However, the function of the Temple, both in the rituals conducted therein and its role as the center of the national cult, requires a different type of investigation. The study of Temple rituals still must rely primarily on the close study of the biblical text and extra-biblical sources of contemporary groups. However, for information on the role of the Temple vis-à-vis local religious practices, archaeology is beginning to offer tantalizing, albeit cautious and preliminary, insights.

In recent years, archaeological research has given form to the Bible's oblique references to local cult places, altars, and temples. From Dan to Beer-sheba, excavations have identified Iron Age areas that have been classified as "cult rooms" or "sanctuaries," and, in one instance, even a "temple." The identification of such cultic areas is based on two lines of evidence: the distinctive plan and architectural elements of areas used for ceremonial purposes, and the presence of specialized artifacts used primarily for the cult. Because cultic areas are sometimes defined solely on the presence of certain types of artifacts, we will focus first on objects associated with the cult.

The objects found in Cult Room 49 at tenth-century Lachish (Level V) exemplify the types of artifacts that are normally interpreted as cultic, i.e., used principally in the performance of religious ceremony. The Cult Room was discovered close to the center of the tell, adjacent to and underlying the "solar shrine" of the later Persian Period. Inside the room, alongside a raised central platform, was found a limestone altar which originally may have had four horns (see no. 1). It is similar in shape and manufacture to stone altars found in over a dozen other sites throughout the Levant during the early part of the Iron Age.

Small altars such as the Lachish example (45 cm. in height) were probably not used for the sacrifice of animals. It is more likely that they were used for the burning of grain, animal fats, wine and oil offerings, as evidenced by the remains of burnt organic material found on altar surfaces. Larger altars, such as one at Arad, may have been used for animal sacrifices, an interpretation supported by a slab of flint encircled by plastered channels on the altar. These channels may have been used to direct the flow of blood after the sacrifice of an animal.

Based on this evidence, altars are believed to have been the central appurtenance of ritual areas. This is also true of other cultures throughout the Near East whose altars, although not of the stone, four-horned variety, occupy the central place in cultic settings. An additional role of Israelite horned altars may have been as a place of asylum for those being pursued by enemies or for revenge.

Artifacts frequently found in close association with altars have also been interpreted as cult objects. Such ceramic artifacts as chalices (nos. 5,6,7) and incense burners (nos. 2,3,4) have thus become signs of cultic activity even when they are found independent of altars.

In an area to the south of Cult Room 49, the excavator found an artificially raised area he classified as a "high place." High places were open-air cultic areas sometimes associated with sacred standing stones (*massebot*). Found in one of two pits located near the Lachish raised platform was the head of a female figurine and two fragments of animal figurines. Such female figurines are frequently connected to images of the fertility goddess Astarte, known throughout the ancient Near East for three millennia. Thus, they may have been used in the hope of ensuring fertility of the soil and of women. Alternative explanations suggest that they are to be seen as the *teraphim* (household gods) mentioned in the Bible (e.g., Genesis 31:19) or as remnants of superstitious beliefs.

Although the Temple in Jerusalem was completed soon after the middle of the tenth century BCE, local places of worship continued to be used by residents of both cities and rural towns. The variation in the architecture, size, and location of cultic areas suggests that religious activities may have taken place on a variety of levels. From our limited evidence, we might tentatively distinguish between three types of cult installations: a small cult room or "cult corner," probably used by single families within domestic contexts; cult areas that were independent structures probably designed specifically for ritual purposes; and local "temples," more formal structures reminiscent of the Temple in Jerusalem.

Examples of small cult rooms have been unearthed at the Galilean city of Megiddo, where cultic objects (chalices and figurines) were discovered in corners of private homes. The profusion of these corners in Megiddo suggests that they were private chapels, perhaps used by individual families.

Cult Room 49 at Lachish may represent an area intended for use by a larger audience than the Megiddo cult corners. Although relatively small, it was not associated with a residential area, and its distinctive architecture, principally the ring of benches around the base of the interior of the walls and the slightly raised central platform, suggests that it was designed specifically for ritual purposes. Larger, perhaps more public, cultic areas have been discovered in or next to the city gates in Megiddo, Beer-sheba, and possibly in Dan. These areas, plus a similar one found outside the walls of Jerusalem, may have been visited by travelers and inhabitants when entering or leaving a settlement. Gate installations were familiar to the biblical writer who mentions "high places of the gates" as being destroyed during the religious reforms of Josiah (II Kgs. 2:8).

Without doubt the most sophisticated cult room so far found in Israel is the Arad "temple." The temple is composed of a large courtyard, two side rooms adjacent to the north side of the court, a main hall, and a small, slightly raised area that has been interpreted as a "Holy of Holies" (the area where priests conducted the holiest of ceremonies). The entrance to the Holy of Holies was flanked by two stone altars, 13 and 17 feet tall respectively. Inside the room was found a stone stele (a sacred standing stone). Based on the architecture of this temple, especially its broad space with a central cella and an altar in the courtyard, it has been compared to the biblical description of the Jerusalem Temple and the Tabernacle constructed by the Israelites in the desert (Ex.27).

The Arad temple was in existence from about the time of Solomon until its destruction in the middle of the seventh century BCE. The excavator of Arad has suggested that a temple was built there because the city was on the border of the Negev desert; it thus served as a religious center for those leaving and entering the country. This explanation could also be applied to the well-developed cultic area found at Dan, which is on the northern boundary of the country.

Two *ostraca* (inscribed pot sherds) found at the Arad temple bear the name of two priestly families known from the Bible. This may be an indication that priests were present at the temple, either as permanent clergy or as part of a rotation of Levitical personnel stationed in Jerusalem. It would then be sensible to assume that the Arad temple operated in concert with the national Temple. It is impossible to say whether other cult places also enjoyed legitimacy as part of the state's religious structure.

We may surmise that the central rite of the public cult areas was the sacrifice of an animal or the burning of meal, wine or oil on the altar. Such offerings may have served the same purposes as those that dominated Temple ritual: the offering of one's best foodstuff was a sign of devotion to God.

Almost all of the small and large cultic areas in Israel disappear before or during the seventh century BCE. Their termination may reflect the reforms of King Josiah (620 BCE), who purged all local priesthoods and cult centers in deference to the Jerusalem Temple, probably as a reaction to the increasingly pagan nature of the local cult areas. It seems that the coexistence of national and local cultic centers was tolerated during the period when the monarchy was first established. Perhaps at that time pagan influences had not yet compromised the Yahwistic nature of the ceremonies. When such influences became increasingly prevalent, the local cult areas were no longer acceptable to the Jerusalem priesthood, and the Jerusalem Temple was projected as the only legitimate place of worship, with all other local cult areas abolished.

Home Life (Nos. 14–52)

The Hebrew word for house, *bayit,* occurs some 2,000 times in the Bible, yet there is not one extensive biblical description of a house plan or of the daily home activities of the family. We may assume that such a description was unnecessary in the eyes of the biblical writer, whose veiled references to doors and windows, to courtyards and spinning areas, were frequently used as simple metaphors, easily understood by the ancient Israelites. But the passage of time has clouded our understanding of these once simple statements; they now are intriguing glimpses of everyday life in ancient Israel that archaeological excavations have fleshed out over the past century.

The basic plan of an Iron Age house consisted of four rooms: an inner and outer courtyard, one room on a side of the courtyard and one room on the back axis running the length of the whole building. This plan was expanded by adding rooms to the side of the courtyard or with a second story. The courtyard was divided into two sections, frequently by one or two rows of

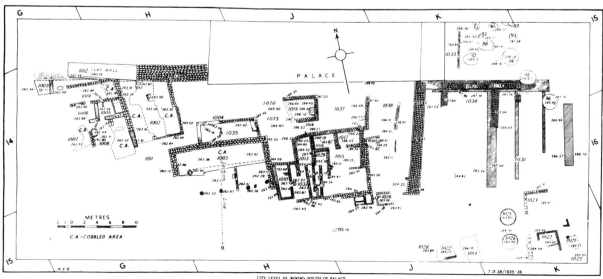

Iron Age Homes

34

pillars. The central part was uncovered, allowing sunlight to filter through the court into the rooms along its perimeter. Household chores that required an air draft, like cooking or baking, took place in the open area. A house found in Lachish, measuring 11 × 10.5 meters, had a courtyard that contained a stone- and mud-brick oven, a quern for the grinding of grain into flour, and two-handled cooking pots, many fire-blackened on the bottom.

Most homes were entered only through the courtyard, an area sometimes shared by many houses on a street. Doors opened inward from the street, as evidenced by a house at Lachish whose doorway was marked by two charred beams on each side of the entrance, possibly remains of the door frame or jambs. The lintel and sill were probably made from wood or stone. Hinges of wood or metal may have been set within pockets or depressions on the lintel and threshold; excavations have recovered the remains of protective metal coverings on hinges and sockets, perhaps designed to prevent wear. Although locks and bolts are mentioned in the Bible (II Sam. 13:17) none have come to light during excavations.

The two rooms that flanked the courtyard were the living and storage areas; some larger homes had three or even four rooms arranged around the court. Generally, one area was set aside for the storage and preparation of food. Jars with narrow necks to prevent evaporation were used to store oil and wine; wide-mouthed jars were used to store dry goods, such as grain and flour. At Lachish, almost every house had at least one storage jar, some found near smaller jugs and juglets that were used to transfer liquids from the large jars into goblets or mugs.

Bowls and dishes, along with mugs and chalices, may have been stored on benches that have been found along the walls of rooms, or on straw mats on the floor. "Pilgrim" flasks, used to hold drinking water, may have hung from the wall in the

bedroom or been placed against the wall in the courtyard or kitchen area. Oil lamps were placed on these benches or in wall niches to provide the only light when the sun no longer illuminated the interior of the house.

An adjacent room might have been the sleeping quarters. People may have slept on straw mats or on slightly raised platforms covered with carpets. The possible use of four-legged beds is attested to by the existence of small clay models of "divan" beds with backs or headboards from the Iron Age. However, no actual furniture has survived from that period and archaeologists can only draw analogues from Bronze Age Jericho (where wooden stools and tables were found in a tomb) and from Egyptian tombs and Assyrian wall reliefs.

Although archaeologists usually only find the bottom-most courses of walls and can only approximate their original height, very wide walls sometimes suggest that a second story was supported. One affluent home from Megiddo had six-foot wide walls and over-all dimensions of 104 × 97 feet. The courtyard on the northeast side of the building contained the remnants of a staircase that probably led to a second floor. In such a structure it is possible that the ground floor became the storage area and the upper floor the living quarters.

Some of the larger houses may have also been used for commercial and industrial as well as domestic activities. At Jericho, one house had narrow booths attached to its exterior walls. The booths contained rows of clay storage jars full of carbonized grain that may have been ground in the many querns found in the house, suggesting a family-based business for the grinding and sale of grain. The production of olive oil seems to have been a main occupation at the rural settlement of Tell Beit Mirsim, based on the frequent occurrence of stone vats used for pressing olives, found in or near private homes.

The part of a city in which a home is located helps the archaeologist to interpret economic and social differentiation within that community. At Tirzah, for example, a wall inside the city separated the larger, better built homes from those that were more poorly constructed. The more affluent homes were on the western edge of the mound where cooling winds from the Mediterranean provided some relief from the scorching sun. An enormous "palace-fort" at Lachish may have been the residence of a regional governor during the city's heyday in the eighth century BCE. The large homes built alongside this palace may have belonged to the city's wealthy class because of their choice locations and large sizes.

From Solomonic times onward certain sites, such as Beer-sheba in the south and Hazor in the north, may have developed into regional capitals. This is reflected in the increased amount of space devoted to administrative buildings and the decreased number of private dwelling units. At Beer-sheba, the excavators estimate that only fifty residential buildings existed on the tell, with most of the population residing in satellite villages around the city. This is also true for many cities occupied over a long period of time, for the amount of habitable space on a tell decreases through the ages. As the mound continues to rise, due to the accumulation of layer after layer, it narrows at the summit. This limits the number of buildings that can be constructed and forces most of the population to live outside of the city walls.

City dwellers must have obtained their agricultural produce from the small farms of single families, located in the hinterlands beyond the tell. Barley and wheat were grown, olives and dates harvested, and sheep and goats kept for wool, milk, and cheese. The daily life of these people was governed by the agricultural seasons, which are described on a ninth- or tenth-century agricultural calendar found at Gezer: "His two months are (olive) harvest, His two months are planting (grain), His two months are late planting; His month is hoeing up of flax, His month is harvest of barley, His month is harvest and feasting; His two months are vine-tending, His month is summer fruit."[1]

While archaeological studies help scholars to reconstruct aspects of ancient economy, living conditions and everyday life, it is much more difficult to discern details of family life and social interactions. Unfortunately, it is almost impossible without inscriptional evidence to reconstruct the fabric of family life, the particular customs that mark the birth, education, and marriage of individuals and the observance of holidays and fasts. We may presume that some of the artifacts uncovered in the home were used for rituals by the family but the content of these ceremonies and the beliefs behind them are rarely apparent from the study of objects alone.

From the Bible we may glean the importance of the family in the maintenance of tradition and the performance of Jewish ritual (I Sam. 20:29; Job 1:5). Although no direct biblical evidence attests to the oral transmission of a collective heritage and history, this is generally assumed to be the purpose of some of the songs and stories preserved in poetry: "Give ear, O my people, to my teaching; Incline your ears to the words of my mouth. I will open my mouth with a parable; I will utter dark sayings concerning days of old. That which we have heard and known, And our fathers have told us, We will not hide from their children, Telling to the generations to come the praises of the Lord, and His strength, and His wondrous works that He hath done" (Psalm 78).

The State of Ancient Israel (Nos. 53–66)

If religion formed the spiritual base of Israelite society, and home life the basic economic and social unit, then the state can be said to have been the most powerful integrative and regulative institution. The

1 Translation by W. F. Albright, *Ancient Near Eastern Texts*, p. 320.

transformation of Israel from a largely tribal organization to a centralized, monarchic state wrought changes in every level of the society. Jerusalem was selected as both the religious and political capital of the new nation, and the country was reorganized into twelve administrative districts to facilitate taxation, regulate commerce, and to further erode tribal boundaries and loyalties. As a state Israel became an international power whose borders extended from the Euphrates River to the border of Egypt. The securing of these boundaries helped to engender a sense of national identity, an identity that was crucial to the survival of the people during the Exile to Babylon.

The extent of the impact of the state on the everyday life of the people was recognized by the prophet Samuel before the anointment of Saul. In response to their pleas for a king, the prophet predicted that the burden of kingship would eventually be borne by their children:

These will be the ways of the king who will reign over you: he will take your sons and appoint them to his chariots and to be his horsemen, and to run before his chariots; and he will appoint for himself commanders of thousands and commanders of fifties, and some to plow his ground and to reap his harvest and to make his implements of war and the equipment of his chariots. He will take your daughters to be perfumers and cooks and bakers, He will take the best of your fields and vineyards and olive orchards and give them to his servants. He will take the tenth of your grain and your vineyards and give it to his officers and servants. He will take your menservants and maidservants and the best of your cattle and your asses and put them to his work. He will take the tenth of your flocks and you shall be his slaves. And in that day you will cry out because of your king. (I Sam. 8)

For the archaeologist, the impact of the formation of a state in Israel is reflected in the sudden appearance of well-built, fortified cities on top of levels that were largely abandoned or were only small settlements. All at once, or so it seems from the archaeological record, Hazor, Megiddo, and Gezer were encircled with defensive walls and protected by monumental city gates whose plans were so similar they could have been built according to the same blueprint.

Many of the larger sites, e.g., Megiddo and Beer-sheba, became regional capitals, as evidenced by the construction of "palaces" or regional headquarters at the highest point of the city. Lachish too was awakened from over a century of dormancy and equipped with a "palace-fort" and bastion; it served perhaps as a storage city while Jerusalem emerged as a capital unparalleled in the history of Canaan. Small sites throughout the Negev were also fortified with double walls, perhaps as a system of fortresses to protect the burgeoning trade routes.

There can be no doubt that these massive building projects required constant infusions of money and labor. For the most part, the burden of supporting the king's works rested on the shoulders of the people. As Solomon's cities grew so did the level of taxation and conscripted labor, along with an ever burgeoning bureaucratic system to oversee the flow of goods and services into the district capitals (see I Kings 4). Many of the court officials were granted tracts of land as payment for their services. This, coupled with the collection of taxes in the form of produce, increasingly placed the control of agriculture under the aegis of the state.

Solomon's ambitious building projects and expanded bureaucracy of civil servants and regional officials did not abate during his forty-year reign. The issues of forced labor and taxation were so heated at the time of his death that they ultimately led to the division of the kingdom into two independent states (I Kings 12).

With the emergence of Israel and Judah as two separate political states, administration of the region was divided between two governments. In the south (Judah), Jerusalem remained the capital; Lachish emerged as a regional capital as evidenced by the expansion of the "palace-fort" to include a ceremonial courtyard.

An important archaeological clue for reconstructing the operation of the Judean state is the hundreds of "stamped" jar handles excavated at Lachish and many other Iron Age sites (see nos. 53–56). These handles were once part of large storage jars that were stamped with seals before firing. The handles found at Lachish came almost exclusively from one level (III) and are all dated to the eighth century BCE. The images on the seal impressions break down into two main types. The first, called royal seals, bear the inscription "[Belonging] to the king," and one of four place names. The second type of seal bears only an inscribed name and is called a private seal, although today scholars interpret it as that of a royal official.

The stamped storage jars are found in sites all over southern Israel. They seem to be associated with the king and his officials, perhaps pertaining in some way to governmental economic administration. Yet scholars have been debating their significance for the past century and have come to no conclusive interpretation of their function. In the case of the royal seal, four main theories have been advanced:

1) The storage jars were used to collect taxes in the form of oil or wine in the four cities named, and shipped to the king.
2) The jars were produced in the four cities mentioned above by private potters who had received royal commissions.
3) The four cities were administrative seats of Judean districts; oil and wine collected in their districts were shipped to the governmental seat for storage and/or distribution.
4) The royal stamp guaranteed the standardized capacity of the vessel.

It is unclear why so many stamped jars were in use at Lachish. If the named towns were points of origin for the jars, then the taxes may have been destined for Lachish where they were stored. If the sites named were the destination, then they may have originated in Lachish and were intended for shipment to one of the storage cities. Perhaps excavation of the four sites named in the seal impressions will shed light on the exact function of these jars.

In the case of the so-called private stamps, scholars now agree that they too are associated with royal business, based on a recent discovery of two complete jars at Lachish, each with four handles impressed with both royal and private stamps. The fact that handles with the same official's stamp have been found at more than one site may also imply centralized production or distribution centers.

While the stamped jar handles elucidate the economic workings of the state, the Lachish Letters (twenty-one inscribed pot sherds) are unusual evidence for communication between cities and the political process of the day. These Letters were found in the level (II) immediately preceding the Babylonian destruction. Although only about one-third are legible, enough can be gleaned to understand something of the military structure of Judah immediately prior to the Babylonian destruction of Lachish.

The *ostraca* were primarily letters written to Yaosh, the military governor of Lachish, perhaps from Hoshayahu, a subordinate officer of Yaosh in one of the outposts near Lachish. The Letters may have been written over a long period of time—they refer to previous communications and events—but seem to come to a climax when Hoshayahu writes:

for the signal-stations of Lachish we are watching according to all the signs which my lord gives, because we do not see the signals of Azekah.

This is strikingly similar to a verse in the Book of Jeremiah (39:7) which lists Jerusalem, Lachish and Azekah as the last surviving strongholds against the Babylonians. Apparently, a system of smoke signals had been arranged among the Judean cities to alert one another to impending invasion, political troubles, or any other event that might need quick action. The lack of signals from Azekah may mean that the city had already fallen to the Babylonians and only Lachish and Jerusalem remained as unconquered fortified cities.

The Lachish Letters also offer insight into the relationship of the military, the government, and religious leaders. One of the Letters contains a reference to a prophet, the only extra-biblical use of this word (Heb. *navi*). Unfortunately, the full name of the prophet has not been preserved; it may have been Jeremiah, Urijah, or any one of the many religious men of that era. Both Jeremiah and Urijah had urged the Jerusalem government to surrender to the Babylonians, an opinion vehemently opposed by royal officials, who denounced Jeremiah, "for he is weakening thehands of the soldiers" (Jer. 38:4). This same expression is used in one of the Lachish Letters, although it refers to one of the officials. Evidently, the government was split into parties loyal to different prophets and priests who offered different advice and visions of the future. The prophet in the Lachish Letters is a messenger who transmits messages between military leaders. His political role is very much in keeping with that of prophets of this time period, especially Jeremiah, and highlights the complex state of affairs that combined political, military and religious interests.

The archaeological evidence for Iron Age Israel reveals a complex society whose members were involved in a mosaic of activities that centered about daily activities in the home, interaction with official doctrines and policies of state, guided by the precepts and laws of their religion. Jerusalem was the center of political and religious life and, both directly and indirectly, the palace controlled economic matters as well. Regional capitals such as Lachish probably were major markets for goods produced by individual families and larger estates. Systems of exchange and taxation were regulated by the state, strengthening ties between the central administration of the state and local villages and families.

With the destruction of the Temple and the capital, the idea of a national state centered in Jerusalem became a symbol of the hope for a renewed religious and political identity. This hope, plus the well-established tradition of the home as a basic transmitter of history and values, enabled the Jews to survive the Exile as a distinct group until the reemergence of the state under the Maccabees some four centuries later.

1. Altar

Megiddo, Stratum V A–IV B, Locus R 12
Iron II A, 10th cent. BCE
Limestone: carved and ground
Ht. 51 cm., max. length and width 32.5 cm.
Loaned by The Oriental Institute, University of
  Chicago, museum no. A 13188, field no. 2983

The use of altars for making offerings to the
deity is known to many cultures of the ancient
Near East, including the Canaanites. However, the
stone altar with horns, such as this example from
Megiddo, seems to be confined to Israel. Horned
altars are described in the Bible, particularly as a
major ritual object in the Jerusalem Temple, and
are attested to archaeologically at many Iron Age
sites throughout Israel.

Large altars could be made of natural rock or
artificial heaps of stones (like the one at Arad),
thereby conforming to the prohibition against
hewing the stone with iron chisels (Ex. 20:22).
However, the small stone altars such as this
example from Megiddo and the one from Cult
Room 49 at Lachish are obviously carved. It is
possible that this injunction did not extend to the
small sanctuary altars, or that iron was not used.

Four basic items were sacrificed on the two altars
in Jerusalem: animals, wine, incense, and grain
meal mixed with oil. During the Iron Age, animal
sacrifice was periodically allowed outside the
Temple and then forbidden (e.g., by the reforms
of Kings Hezekiah and Josiah). Limestone altars
like the one shown here were probably too small
to be used for animal sacrifice, although at Tell
Qiri the remains of the ritual animal portions
allotted to the priests were found in a cult room.

Offerings were required by biblical injunction to
be made by the priests twice daily (Ex. 29:38–43)
and on the three major holidays of Passover
(*Pesach*), the Feast of Weeks (*Shavuot*) and the
Feast of Tabernacles (*Sukkot*) (Num. 28–29). In
addition, they were made on behalf of individuals
who wished to give thanks, proffer devotion,
request aid, or expiate sins and offenses (de Vaux
1961: 414–421). It is likely that these individual
offerings were performed in the small
sanctuaries and cult corners outside Jerusalem.

Description: square pedestal; horizontal molding with
square edges above pedestal midpoint; central
depression in top; originally one horn on each corner
(only two recovered).
Bibliography: *Megiddo Cult:* 12–13, pl. XII:2983.
Parallels: *Megiddo Cult:* pl. XII:2984, M4555, M5331,
M5154, 2982; *Lachish V:* pl. 27:3.

1

The Cult Stand

The Bible mentions that the Tabernacle in the
desert and the Temple in Jerusalem had two
altars, one for the burnt offering and the other
for incense. It is possible that in small sanctuaries
the stone altar (no. 1) served the former function,
while ceramic cultic stands, several found fitted
with bowls, were used for burning incense, since
the two types are often found together.

These cylindrical stands are not unique to the
Israelite cult, but also were part of Canaanite
ritual, as attested to by a fourth-millennium
example from Beer-sheba (Amiran 1970: photo
331) and a second-millennium stand from Lachish
(Amiran 1970: photo 339). Several stands have
bowls attached, while in other instances the
stands have been found near bowls with fire-
blackened insides (*Lachish V:* fig. 6). Bowls found
at Megiddo (cf. no. 4) and Lachish have curious
conical projections as decoration and have funnel-
like tubes attached below. It is not clear how the
stand and bowl apparatus might have functioned,
and probably only the fenestrated variety of
stand could have contained a fire below. The

funnel-like bowls set on unfenestrated stands may alternatively have served for the libation of wine, which had to be poured out completely inside the sanctuary (Num. 28:7).

Incense was burned twice a day on the Jerusalem altar and was also supplemental to other types of offerings: with grain, with the first fruits, and with the showbread. Another method of incense offering was to place it in a censer. The censer was taken into the Holy of Holies on the Day of Atonement by the priest (Lev. 16:12–13).

2. Fenestrated Cult Stand

Beth Shan, Level V, Room 1028
Iron II A, ca. 1050 BCE
Clay: wheel-turned, rolled handles, slipped, painted, fired
Ht. 60 cm., diam. at rim 16 cm., diam. at base
  21.8 cm.
Loaned by The University Museum, University of
  Pennsylvania 29–103–818

Description: cylindrical hollow body, narrowing toward the top; two vertical loop handles on each side (one restored); two oval openings in body between handles. Brown ware; brown slip; purple painted decoration in horizontal bands on rim, shoulder, and body below handles, vertical lines on body.
Bibliography: Rowe 1940: pl. 61A:1, pl. 15:3.
Parallels: *Lachish V:* pl. 26:3,6; *Megiddo Cult:* pl. 20: P6055; Amiran 1970: photo 336 (Nahariya), photo 345 (Beth Shan).

3. Cult Stand (NOT ILLUSTRATED)

Megiddo, Stratum IV, Locus O 14:331
Iron II A, 10th–9th cent. BCE
Clay: wheel-turned and fired
Ht. 25 cm., diam. 12.3 cm.
Loaned by The Oriental Institute, University of
  Chicago, museum no. A 13464, field no. 2803

Description: hollow cylindrical stand, narrowing toward top, which is broken off; foot flares. Mottled yellow- to pink-buff ware.
Bibliography: *Megiddo Cult:* pl. XIX:2803.
Parallels: *Lachish V:* pl. 26:4,5.

4. Funneled Bowl Fragment
(NOT ILLUSTRATED)
Megiddo, Stratum V, Locus S 10=1671
Late Iron I, ca. 1050–1000 BCE
Clay: wheel-turned, applied decoration, burnished,
  painted, fired
Ht. 11 cm., width 14.6 cm.
Loaned by The Oriental Institute, University of
  Chicago, museum no. A 28457, field no. P 5803

Description: fragmentary bowl, convex-sided with strongly everted rim; conical projections around midpoint; hole in bottom of bowl empties into long, cylindrical hollow tube, like a funnel, with hole in bottom. Yellow- to pink-buff ware; five red-brown painted bands on interior; burnished interior and exterior; fire-blackening on interior.
Bibliography: *Megiddo Cult:* pl. XIX:P 5803.
Parallels: *Megiddo Cult:* fig. 7; *Lachish V:* pl. 26:1,2.

2

The Chalice

Chalices are bowls on high pedestal stands that traditionally have been interpreted as ceremonial objects based on their association with altars. They are found in Israel during the Bronze and Iron Ages, although not always in religious contexts. In the Iron Age, for example, at Lachish, Cult Room 49 (10th century) contained seven chalices in association with a stone altar and four incense stands; but additional chalices were also found in tombs, caves used as dwellings, and domestic rooms.

We cannot reconstruct the exact function of the chalice in sanctuary, tomb, or home on purely archaeological grounds. The name "chalice" was probably given by archaeologists because of the resemblance of the shape to the medieval form. Libations of wine accompanying other offerings were an important part of Tabernacle and Temple ritual mentioned in the Bible (Num. 15:1–12, 28:7). It is therefore conceivable that the chalices can be associated with this aspect of Jewish ceremony.

5. Chalice

Israel
Iron II A–C, 1000–600 BCE
Clay: wheel-turned and fired
Ht. 14 cm., diam. 16.1 cm.
Purchased in Israel, 1981
Gift of the Betty and Max Ratner Collection   1982–14

The form of this chalice, with its simple, flaring rim and gently carinated bowl, closely parallels one from Lachish Cult Room 49 (10th century).

Description: flaring rim with rounded edge; shallow bowl with vertical sides and gentle carination at bottom converging toward the stem; cylindrical hollow stem flares into a wide foot. Orange ware.
Parallels: *Lachish III:* pl. 83:158,160; *Lachish V:* pl. 42:17.

6. Chalice (NOT ILLUSTRATED)

Lachish, Tomb 1002
Iron II B–C, 900–700 BCE
Clay: wheel-turned and fired
Ht. 15.5 cm., diam. 19.9 cm.
Archaeology Acquisition Fund   JM 12–73.126

The wide, horizontal carinated rim of this chalice is characteristic of the types from southern Israel.

Description: wide, everted, horizontal rim with carinated edges; vertical-sided bowl carinated at bottom; cylindrical hollow stem, foot missing. Orange ware.
Bibliography: *Lachish III:* pl. 83:162.

5

7. Chalice

Israel
Iron I, 1200–1000 BCE
Clay: wheel-turned and fired
Ht. 17.3 cm., diam. 20.2 cm.
Purchased in Israel
Gift of the Betty and Max Ratner Collection   1981–155

Description: wide, everted rim; convex-sided bowl
with high carination; hollow stem with rounded step
near base and wide, flaring foot. Mottled orange and
buff ware; modern repair on foot.
Bibliography: Kozloff 1978: no. RC 113, fig. 32.
Parallels: Amiran 1970: pl. 68:7 (Beth Shemesh), pl.
68:8 (Tell Qasile).

7

8. Jug

Lachish, Tomb 106
Iron II A–C, 1000–586 BCE
Clay: wheel-turned, pulled handle, slipped, wheel-
  burnished, fired
Ht. 23.5 cm., diam. 17.5 cm.
Archaeology Acquisition Fund   JM 12–73.298

This cylindrical-necked jug is very similar to one
found in Lachish Cult Room 49 (10th century).
Typological differences include the presence of
an inner ledge on the rim and of ridges on the
handle in the Jewish Museum jug. Although the
latter was found in Tomb 106, dated to the
7th–6th centuries BCE, its form appears to have
originated several centuries earlier.

Description: wide, cylindrical neck joins sharply with
tall, convex-sided body; narrow ring base; rim vertical
on exterior, with interior ledge; handle has
hemispherical cross-section with three vertical ridges.
Orange ware; buff slip.
Bibliography: *Lachish III:* pl. 85:205.
Parallels: *Lachish V:* pl. 24:5, pl. 42:6; Amiran 1970:
pl. 87:1 (Tell Farah South); *Beer-sheba I:* pl. 54:15,16.

8

9

10

9. Two-handled Cooking Pot

Israel
Iron II A–B, 1000–800 BCE
Clay: wheel-turned, pulled handles, fired
Ht. 12.2 cm., diam. 17.5 cm.
Purchased in Israel
Gift of Joy Ungerleider, 1968   JM 246–68

Archaeologists have been able to interpret the function of cooking pots because many have heavy fire-blackening on their outer surfaces (as does this pot), indicative of their placement in the fire. Cooking pots, generally found in Iron Age homes and tombs, were also discovered in Lachish Cult Room 49 and possibly served in the preparation of offerings for the altar. The squat, carinated form and two handles of this vessel suggest it can be dated to the first two centuries of the first millennium BCE.

Description: squat, biconical body carinated at midpoint; concave-sided neck with carinated step below rim; rim converging with exterior thickened molding; round base; two opposing handles with oval cross-section. Brown ware; fire-blackened on bottom and one side.
Parallels: Amiran 1970: pl. 76:7 (Beth Shemesh); *Beer-sheba I:* pl. 53:CP 50.

10. Bowl

Lachish, Tomb 116
Iron II A–B, 1000–800 BCE
Clay: wheel-turned, slipped, fired
Ht. 7.6 cm., diam. 19.5 cm.
Archaeology Acquisition Fund   JM 12–73.110

This sharply carinated bowl with vertical sides came from Tomb 116 at Lachish, which the excavator dated to ca. 875 BCE. A bowl of very similar shape was found in Cult Room 49 of Lachish and at 9th- and 8th-century strata at Beer-sheba, indicating that the form was produced for several centuries during the early first millennium BCE.

Description: near-vertical-sided bowl, carinated at midpoint and converging sharply to narrow ring base; second slight carination midway between rim and main carination; vertical rim, slightly thickened on exterior and interior. Mottled orange and buff ware; tan core; red slip on interior to exterior of rim; three wheel-incised bands on lower exterior.
Bibliography: *Lachish III:* pl. 79:26.
Parallels: *Lachish V:* pl. 23:9, pl. 41:5; *Beer-sheba I:* pl. 56:10, pl. 59:49; Amiran 1970: pl. 63:3 (Beth Shemesh).

11   12

11. Juglet

Israel
Iron II A–B, 1000–800 BCE
Clay: wheel-turned, rolled handle, slipped, hand-
  burnished, fired
Ht. 9.8 cm., diam. 6.1 cm.
Purchased in Israel
Gift of Joy Ungerleider, 1968   JM 243–68

Juglets such as this probably were dipped into
large storage jars in order to fill serving jugs,
bowls, or lamps. In cultic installations they may
have been used for filling the oil lamps, chalices,
or jugs, such as those found in Cult Room 49.

Description: low globular body; tall neck with
straight sides diverging toward rim; rim straight
exterior and interior; handle round in cross-section;
button disc base. Pink-red ware; pink slip on exterior;
hand-burnished.
Parallels: *Lachish V:* pl. 25:4, pl. 42:9; Amiran 1970:
photo 263.

12. Pinched-mouth Juglet

Lachish, Tomb 116
Iron II A–B, 1000–800 BCE
Clay: wheel-turned, pulled handle, slipped, hand-
  burnished, fired
Ht. 10.4 cm., diam. 6.5 cm.
Archaeology Acquisition Fund   JM 12–73.205

Description: globular body; tall, cylindrical neck,
pinched at top to form spout; rim vertical, thickened
on exterior and interior; handle has round cross-
section with vertical ridge on underside; round base.
Orange ware; exterior red slip absent in handle area;
irregular hand-burnish is horizontal on body and
vertical on neck.
Parallels: *Lachish III:* pl. 88:288; *Lachish V:* pl. 25:3.

13. Oil Lamp

Lachish, Tomb 1002
Iron II C, 800–586 BCE
Clay: wheel-turned and fired
Ht. 4.1 cm., diam. 12.5 cm.
Archaeology Acquisition Fund   JM 12–73.58

The oil was placed in the bowl, and the wick, usually made of flax, protruded from the spout, as evidenced by the fire-blackening on the spouts of most lamps. The cult lamps of the Temple, and possibly those of the sanctuaries, had to contain pure olive oil (Ex. 27:19–20; Lev. 24:2). Whether the lamps found in small sanctuaries functioned as eternal lights (as prescribed for the Temple), for some kind of lighting ceremony, or merely as light sources is undetermined.

The lamp shown here comes from a tomb that the excavator dated to the 8th century BCE.

However, its form is similar to a 10th-century lamp from Lachish Cult Room 49, and the depth of the bowl, the narrowness of the everted rim, and the width and height of the spout suggest that this may be an earlier Iron Age form.

The transition from open bowls with four pinched spouts to those with one folded spout occurred in the early second millennium BCE, and this basic form continued with variations in style until the Hellenistic Period.

Description: deep bowl with carination at the everted, narrow rim; pinch of spout is blunt with wide gap between edges; base round. Orange ware; fire-blackened spout.
Bibliography: *Lachish III:* pl. 83, possibly Type 144 or 146.
Parallels: *Lachish V:* pl. 42:12; Amiran 1970: pl. 100:11.

13

14. Two-handled Cooking Pot

Lachish, Tomb 106
Iron II C, 800–586 BCE
Clay: wheel-turned, neck grooved, handle
  pulled and incised, slipped, hand-burnished, fired
Ht. 17.3 cm., diam. 16.8 cm.
Archaeology Acquisition Fund   JM 12–73.167

Cooking vessels of this rounded form with tall, grooved necks were particularly numerous in the domestic rooms of Lachish Level III (800–700 BCE), and less so in those of Level II (700–586 BCE). They are easily distinguishable from the carinated cooking pots of the Iron II A–B Period. The cross incised into the handle may be the Proto-Sinaitic letter *tav* and is possibly a potter's mark (*Lachish III:* 346; *Lachish V:* 17). Since the same sign is found in cooking pots at other southern sites, it would be of interest to study their distribution pattern. If the mark is indeed a potter's mark, one might be able to locate the workshop of a specific potter and learn how his or her products were marketed at other sites. However, it is also possible that the marks were meant to distinguish the pot for a special purpose. A study of the types of contexts they appear in might provide insight into this hypothesis.

Description: tall, cylindrical neck with five horizontal grooves; carinated ridge at join of neck and shoulder; globular body, widest point near rounded base; rim vertical, slightly thickened on exterior to form molding; handles: oval cross-section, incised cross on one. Mottled red-orange and buff ware; red core; irregular burnish marks on base.
Bibliography: *Lachish III:* pl. 93:456 (although this type is not recorded from Tomb 106).
Parallels: *Lachish V:* pl. 53:CP 150, pl. 35:6,8; *Amiran 1970:* pl. 76:15 (Beit Mirsim); *Beer-sheba I:* pl. 56:14; pl. 61:96,97.

15. Two-handled Cooking Pot
(NOT ILLUSTRATED)

Israel
Iron II C, 800–586 BCE
Clay: wheel-turned, pulled handle, neck grooved, fired
Ht. 13.1 cm., diam. 13.1 cm.
Purchased in Jerusalem, 1981
Gift of the Betty and Max Ratner Collection   1982–4

Description: cylindrical neck with three horizontal grooves, carinated ridge where neck meets body; convex-sided body with vertical mid-section; round bottom; rim vertical and sharp-edged; handles have oval cross-section (one is a recent replacement); two sets of double wheel-made bands on shoulder. Orange-red for ancient ware; replaced handle buff ware; black core; surface fire-blackened in places.
Parallels: *Lachish III:* pl. 93:452; *Amiran 1970:* pl. 76:15 (Beit Mirsim); *Beer-Sheba I:* pl. 70:10.

16. Large Spouted Bowl

Lachish, Area 100
Possibly Late Bronze Age to Iron I, 1550–1000 BCE
Clay: wheel-turned, rolled handle, slipped, fired
Ht. 14.2 cm., diam. 24.8 cm.
Archaeology Acquisition Fund   JM 12–73.134

This large bowl once had an added spout opposite its handle. The spout has since broken off, exposing the core of clay below and the round hole smoothed in the bowl wall through which its contents were poured. The blackening in the interior of the bowl suggests that it may have been used for cooking or burning. The bowl is perhaps an earlier Iron Age or even Late Bronze Age form. It was published as a unique type with the Iron Age material from Lachish and labeled as "miscellaneous." However it is unclear what its assigned provenance of "100" refers to; area 100 contained a series of Late Bronze Age temples and Iron Age burials. Stylistically, based on the shape and buff slip, the bowl belongs somewhere in the Late Bronze Age to Iron I range.

Description: convex-sided tall bowl with carination above midpoint, tapering to narrow base; rim vertical on interior, rolled exterior; two horizontal ridges below rim; handle is flat with oval cross-section; disc base; spout broken away, exposing circular area of dark unfired surface; blackened interior of bowl. Orange ware; traces of buff slip.
Bibliography: *Lachish III:* pl. 81:113.
Parallels: *Lachish II:* pl. 43A,B:150; *Beth Shan:* pl. 52:20; *Gezer II:* pl. 30:11. For spouted bowls: *Gezer II:* pl. 8:10.

17. Bowl with Horizontal Ledge Rim

Lachish, Tomb 106
Iron II C, 800–586 BCE
Clay: wheel-turned, slipped, wheel-burnished, fired
Ht. 3.9 cm., diam. 5.8 cm.
Archaeology Acquisition Fund   JM 12–73.109

Description: vertical sides with carination close to rim; rim has vertical interior and everted exterior, forming a horizontal ledge; low disc base. Orange ware; orange core; red slip on interior and rim edge; spiral wheel-burnish on interior and rim edge.
Bibliography: *Lachish III:* pl. 79:37.
Parallels: *Lachish V:* pl. 52:B 450; *Gezer II:* pl. 33:26, pl. 35:18,19,23 for rim.

14

16

17

18

18. Bowl with Everted Rim

Lachish, Tomb 106
Iron II C, 800–700 BCE
Clay: wheel-turned and fired
Ht. 5 cm., diam. 17 cm.
Archaeology Acquisition Fund   JM 12–73.99

Description: convex-sided body; rim everted on
interior and exterior forming ledge with sharp edge;
disc base. Buff ware and core; interior streaked with
brown, possibly a slip.
Bibliography: *Lachish III:* pl. 79:51.
Parallels: Amiran 1970: pl. 65:15 (Beit Mirsim); *Gezer
II:* pl. 34:22.

19. Bowl with Molded Rim

Lachish, Tomb 106
Iron II C, 800–700 BCE
Clay: wheel-turned, slipped, wheel-burnished, fired
Ht. 8.1 cm., diam. 21.6 cm.
Archaeology Acquisition Fund   JM 12–73.115

Description: convex-sided body with slight carination
near rim; inverted rim with exterior thickening;
shallow ring base. Mottled orange and buff ware; red
slip on interior to rim exterior; spiral wheel-burnish on
interior.
Bibliography: *Lachish III:* pl. 80:75.
Parallels: Amiran 1970: pl. 65:3 (Beit Mirsim); *Beer-
sheba I:* pl. 41:13,14, pl. 59:69; *Gezer II:* pl. 36:10,11.

20. Bowl with Horizontal Ledge Rim

Lachish, Tomb 1002
Iron II C, 800–700 BCE
Clay: wheel-turned, slipped, wheel-burnished, fired
Ht. 6.15 cm., diam. 23.3 cm.
Archaeology Acquisition Fund   JM 12–73.91

Description: bowl with diverging straight sides
carinated below midpoint; rim vertical on interior,
everted on exterior, forming horizontal ledge; ring
base. Orange ware; buff core; orange slip on interior
and rim edge; spiral wheel-burnish on interior.
Bibliography: *Lachish III:* pl. 79:47.
Parallels: Amiran 1970: pl. 65:14,15 (Beit Mirsim);
Beer-sheba I: pl. 74:8; *Gezer II:* pl. 32:26.

19

21

22

21. Thin-ware Bowl

Lachish, Tomb 106
Iron II C, 800–700 BCE
Clay: wheel-turned, slipped, fired
Ht. 5.1 cm., diam. 11.7 cm.
Archaeology Acquisition Fund   JM 12–73.95

Description: straight diverging sides with carination near low disc base; rim sharp and straight-sided. Variegated ware: orange and buff on rim, orange on body, brown from base to carination; red slip on interior, buff slip on rim exterior.
Bibliography: *Lachish III:* pl. 79: combination of Types 16 and 45.
Parallels: Amiran 1970: pl. 65:8 (Beth Shemesh); *Beersheba I:* pl. 68:11, pl. 69:8,11.

22. Thin-ware Bowl

Lachish, Tomb 106
Iron II C, 800–700 BCE
Clay: wheel-turned, slipped, fired
Ht. 5.25 cm., diam. 13.3 cm.
Archaeology Acquisition Fund   JM 12–73.96

Description: straight, diverging sides flare slightly more near rim; carination near low disc base; rim sharp and straight-sided. Orange ware; red slip on interior and traces on exterior.
Bibliography: *Lachish III:* pl. 79: combination of Types 16 and 45.
Parallels: Amiran 1970: pl. 65:8 (Beth Shemesh); *Beersheba I:* pl. 68:2,12, pl. 69:8,11.

23

24

23. Large Plate

Lachish, Tomb 106
Iron II C, 800–586 BCE
Clay: wheel-turned, slipped, wheel-burnished, fired
Ht. 7 cm., diam. 27.4 cm.
Archaeology Acquisition Fund   JM 12–73.90

Description: straight, diverging sides; rim straight on interior, everted on exterior, creating wide flat ledge; ring base. Orange ware; buff core; red slip on interior and rim; spiral wheel-burnish on interior.
Bibliography: *Lachish III:* pl. 80:65.
Parallels: *Lachish III:* pl. 80:63; *Beer-sheba I:* pl. 41:5, pl. 74:3.

24. Small Plate

Lachish, Tomb 106
Iron II C, 800–586 BCE
Clay: wheel-turned, slipped, wheel-burnished, fired
Ht. 3 cm., diam. 16.6 cm.
Archaeology Acquisition Fund   JM 12–73.65

Description: straight, diverging sides with slight carination near rim; rim straight on interior and exterior with flat upper surface; disc base. Pink ware; red slip on interior and rim edge; spiral wheel-burnish on interior.
Bibliography: *Lachish III:* pl. 80:64.
Parallels: *Beer-sheba I:* pl. 41:6.

25

25. Small Jug

Lachish, Tomb 1002
Iron II C, 800–700 BCE
Clay: wheel-turned, rolled handle, fired
Ht. 11.5 cm., diam. 10.5 cm.
Archaeology Acquisition Fund   JM 12–73.138

Small jugs with wide mouths and handles may have been used as drinking vessels (*Lachish III:* 289). It is also conceivable that the small thin-ware bowls and the chalices were intended for this same purpose (e.g., nos. 5–7, 21, 22).

Description: wide mouth, short cylindrical neck and near-cylindrical body, slightly wider at the shoulder; inverted rim with exterior thickening and carination where it meets the neck to form molding; body carinated at bottom; base slightly rounded; handle oval in cross-section. Mottled orange and gray ware.
Bibliography: *Lachish III:* pl. 84:182.
Parallels: *Beer-sheba I:* pl. 45:4.

26. Spouted Strainer Jug

Israel
Iron II A–C, 1000–700 BCE
Clay: wheel-turned, handle and spout hand-made, pierced, slipped, hand-burnished, fired
Ht. 23.4 cm., diam. 15.1 cm., spout length 8 cm.
Purchased in Israel
Gift of Joy Ungerleider, 1968   JM 233–68

The function of these strainer vessels is not easy to reconstruct. It is possible that the material to be strained was placed in the trough-like spout and the clear liquid allowed to drip into the vessel (*Lachish III:* 320). If the liquid and solid material were placed inside the jug, it would be too difficult to clean out the solid residue from the inside through the narrow neck. An alternative explanation for the function of these strainer vessels is that they were used for the drinking of a liquid which needed to be strained. Similar spouted sieve jugs, with longer and narrower straw-like spouts, have been excavated from the wealthier tombs of the Phrygian city of Gordion in Turkey. These were in use from the 8th through the 4th centuries BCE and were modeled after second-millennium Anatolian prototypes. Textual sources indicate that the Phrygians drank an unrefined type of beer through straws, and it has been suggested that the spouted strainer jugs were used for this purpose (Sams 1977: 109).

We have no textual evidence that the ancient Israelites brewed beer, although they did grow barley, and beer-drinking was known among their Mesopotamian and Egyptian neighbors. The position of the handle at a right angle to the spout in both the Phrygian and Israelite jugs does facilitate drinking from the spout.

Description: globular body with slight carination below midpoint; trough-like spout extends upward with fourteen strainer holes in body where spout joins; tall, narrow, concave-sided neck with horizontal ridge above midpoint; rim inverted on interior and exterior, with exterior thickening to form triangular molded lip; ring base; handle at right angle to spout, cross-section lentoid. Orange ware; red slip from rim to body carination; vertical hand-burnishing on one-half the vessel; may possibly have been re-burnished in recent times because burnish tracks through and removes accretions.
Parallels: *Lachish III:* pl. 89:364; *Beth Shan:* fig. 23:10, fig. 56:7, fig. 125:5.

27

28

27. Jug with Molded Rim

Lachish, Tomb 1002
Iron II C, 800–700 BCE
Clay: wheel-turned, pulled handle, slipped, fired
Ht. 18.1 cm., diam. 13.2 cm.
Archaeology Acquisition Fund   JM 12–73.151

This type of round-bottomed jug, but with a plain rim, is found at numerous sites dating from ca. 1000–586 BCE. It is very common at Lachish in the 10th through 8th centuries.

Description: globular body; tall, wide concave-sided neck sharply joined with body; rim inverted on interior and exterior with exterior thickening forming triangular molding; handle has hemispherical cross-section; round base. Orange ware; red slip.
Bibliography: *Lachish III:* pl. 84:190.
Parallels: *Beer-sheba I:* pl. 40:2, pl. 55:17, pl. 44:7, pl. 56:8, pl. 69:1, pl. 64:12.

28. Decanter

Israel
Iron II C, 800–586 BCE
Clay: wheel-turned, pulled handle, slipped, wheel-burnished, fired
Ht. 27.3 cm., diam. 18.9 cm.
Provenance lost, excavation no. V 1245
Archaeology Acquisition Fund   JM 12–73.145

Inscriptional evidence has enabled archaeologists to reconstruct that at least one product decanters were used for was wine. One possible translation of an inscription on a decanter from Lachish suggests it stored dark or smoked wine (Ussishkin 1978: 83–84). A second Lachish decanter bears the inscription "extract (or wine) of black raisins" (Lemaire 1980). Raisin wine was also known from the 8th century BCE in Greece, is mentioned in the Babylonian Talmud, and was made by Palestinian Arabs until the beginning of this century.

Description: tall, narrow concave-sided neck with horizontal ridge at midpoint, flaring toward rim; downward sloping shoulder has carinated join with piriform body, which has widest diameter near base; rim everted on interior and exterior, forming a rolled, molded lip; ring base; handle oval in cross-section with vertical groove down center. Mottled orange and buff ware; traces of red slip; horizontal wheel-burnish on body and shoulder.
Parallels: *Lachish III:* pl. 87:273,274,276; *Beer-sheba I:* pl. 62:102, pl. 74:17,18; Amiran 1970: photo 259 (Lachish).

29. Decanter (NOT ILLUSTRATED)

Lachish, Tomb 106
Iron II C, 800–586 BCE
Clay: wheel-turned, pulled handle, slipped, wheel-
  burnished, fired
Ht. 17.6 cm., diam. 11.1 cm.
Archaeology Acquisition Fund   JM 12–73.263

Description: tall, narrow flaring neck, with
horizontal ridge at midpoint; shoulder nearly
horizontal with indentation on one side; carinated join
with body; body nearly cylindrical but widens toward
base; rim has straight interior, everted exterior,
forming molded lip with sharp edge; ring base; handle
oval in cross-section with central vertical groove.
Mottled orange, red, and buff ware; horizontal wheel-
burnish on upper body, shoulder, upper neck and rim,
and vertical on lower back.
Bibliography: *Lachish III:* pl. 87:276 (however, the
excavator does not list any examples of Type 276 for
Tomb 106; our classification therefore differs from
hers).
Parallels: *Beer-sheba I:* pl. 62:102.

30. Pilgrim Flask

Israel
Iron II C, 800–586 BCE
Clay: wheel-turned, pulled handles, wheel-burnished,
  fired
Ht. 31.7 cm., width 22.5 cm.
Purchased in Israel
Gift of the Betty and Max Ratner Collection
  1981–162

Pilgrim flasks, with their globular, often flattened
bodies and two handles, first appeared in Israel
during the Late Bronze Age, ca. 1550 BCE, and
continued to be used at least through Byzantine
times. Their method of manufacture was
unusual. The two halves of the body were
thrown separately on the wheel, like two bowls,
and then joined together. The neck was thrown
separately and applied, and the two handles were
pulled.

These flasks probably held water, and the flatter
ones are reminiscent of the water canteens of
today. A quotation from much later times
mentions that the form called the *kiton*, probably
similar to the pilgrim flask (Zevulun and Olenik
1979: 19–20), was used as a portable liquid
container by travelers (Babylonian Talmud *Baba
Metzia* 62:1). The three knobs below the handle
on this Jewish Museum example are interpreted
as imitations of rivets, as might be found on
metal vessels.

Description: globular body, wider from front to back
than from handle to handle, knob in center of front
and back face, three knobs below each handle; tall,
concave-sided neck with wide, lopsided flare at rim;
rim has vertical sides with two incised horizontal
bands, forming a bowl-like mouth; flat handles, with
two vertical ridges, attached to each other on either
side of neck via a horizontal ridge; base round. Buff
ware; wheel-burnish on front and back of body in
concentric circles.
Bibliography: Kozloff 1978: no. RC 120, fig. 28.
Parallels: *Lachish III:* pl. 76:13, pl. 72:431; *Beer-
sheba I:* pl. 45:15, pl. 63:132; Amiran 1970: pl. 95:12 (Tell
Jemmeh).

31. Amphoriskos

Lachish, Tomb 1002
Iron II C, 800–700 BCE
Clay: wheel-turned, pulled handles, slipped, fired, painted
Ht. 20.1 cm., diam. 9.9 cm.
Archaeology Acquisition Fund   JM 12–73.443

These small jars, which imitate the form of larger storage jars or amphorae, are known from the Late Bronze Age (Amiran 1970: 142, 256) and thus represent one of the many continuations of Canaanite shapes into the Israelite ceramic repertory (such as the pilgrim flask, no. 30, and lotus-seed beads, no. 48).

Description: conical body tapers to button base, horizontal groove at midpoint; concave-sided neck; carination at join between neck and body; rim plain and flared; handles have oval profile. Orange ware; red slip on exterior and on neck interior; two black horizontal bands with white fill at midpoint, base of neck and below rim.
Bibliography: *Lachish III:* pl. 91:424.
Parallels: *Lachish V:* pl. 45:18; *Beer-sheba I:* pl. 67:1, pl. 72:17, pl. 74:16; Amiran 1970: pl. 83:14 (Beit Mirsim).

32. Juglet

Lachish, Tomb 106
Iron II C, 800–586 BCE
Clay: wheel-turned, rolled handle, slipped, fired
Ht. 6 cm., diam. 4.8 cm.
Archaeology Acquisition Fund   JM 12–73.250

Black-ware juglets of this type were very common in the Lachish domestic rooms of Levels III and II (800–586 BCE). Their small size makes it likely that they would have been dipped into narrow-necked storage jars to remove portions of their liquid contents; they have thus been called oil flasks (Negev 1980: 250). This is tentatively confirmed by a quick survey of their find spots at Lachish, which indicates that 69% of the rooms with this juglet type also had narrow-necked storage jars. Another possible use of these flasks was as containers of perfumed oil.

Description: globular body; narrow neck with concave sides; rim straight-sided and flared; handle cross-section round; slightly pointed base. Gray-black ware; black slip.
Bibliography: *Lachish III:* pl. 88:309.
Parallels: *Beer-sheba I:* pl. 45:10, pl. 62:126–128; Amiran 1970: pl. 89:22 (Beit Mirsim), photo 264 (Beth Shemesh).

31

32

33

33. Storage Jar

Israel
Iron II C, 800–586 BCE
Clay: wheel-turned, pulled handles, fired
Ht. 40 cm., diam. 25.7 cm.
Purchased in Israel, 1981
Gift of the Betty and Max Ratner Collection   1982-23

Storage jars with narrow mouths, such as this Jewish Museum jar, were probably used to hold wine and oil so as to minimize evaporation. Wider-mouthed jars contained grains, fruits, and vegetables. Both types were quite common in Iron Age homes and storerooms, but are rarely found in tombs. Because their bottoms are pointed, they probably were placed on pottery stands. Several clay and chalk stoppers, discovered in the Lachish excavations beside a storage jar, indicate how these jars were closed.

The heavy white incrustation on our jar, made of calcium carbonate (limestone) is frequently found on artifacts from Israel and is the result of the chemical make-up of the soil and its interaction with water.

Description: ovoid body, widest point below midpoint, tapers to base with rounded point; low cylindrical neck converges slightly toward rim; sloping shoulder has carinated join with body; vertical straight rim with flattened edge; two handles have wide central ridge and oval cross-section. Reddish ware.

Parallels: Zemer 1977: nos. 5, 6; *Lachish V:* pl. 48:8,9,16; *Beer-sheba I:* pl. 74:6, *Lachish III:* pl. 94:468,476.

34

35

34. Pinched-mouth Juglet

Lachish, Tomb 1002
Iron II C, 800–700 BCE
Clay: wheel-turned, pulled handle, slipped, hand-
  burnished, fired
Ht. 13.9 cm., diam. 7.5 cm.
Archaeology Acquisition Fund   JM 12–73.192

Description: cylindrical body; cylindrical neck flares
slightly to join sloping shoulder; rim flared slightly,
straight sides and rounded edge, one end pinched
slightly to form spout; handle oval in cross-section;
slightly pointed base. Orange ware; orange slip; vertical
hand-burnishing on entire vessel.
Bibliography: *Lachish III:* pl. 88: combination of
Types 286 and 287.
Parallels: *Beer-sheba I:* pl. 55:14, pl. 45:8, pl. 62:115;
Amiran 1970: pl. 87:11 (Beit Mirsim).

35. Spouted Juglet

Israel
Iron II A–C, 1000–586 BCE
Clay: wheel-turned, pulled handle, applied spout,
  burnished, fired, painted
Ht. 13.7 cm., diam. 9 cm.
Purchased in Israel
Gift of Joy Ungerleider, 1968   JM 249–68

Conical-spouted juglets with side handles are
found in numerous sites in Israel (such as Beth
Shan, Lachish, Megiddo) and date from ca. 1000–
586 BCE. However, the barrel shape and painted-
band decoration of this juglet are more unusual
for this type. An excellent parallel for the shape
comes from an Iron Age tomb at Diban in
Jordan, and a parallel for the decoration at
Megiddo.

Description: convex-sided body, conical spout
attached at midpoint, with clay lump at upper
attachment; concave-sided neck, upper part slightly
convex to form a bowl-like mouth; rim has straight
sides and continues the flare of the neck; handle has
circular cross-section with vertical ridge, attached at
right angle to spout and below rim; base flat. Orange
ware; black and white horizontal painted bands below
body midpoint, vertical hand-burnishing on body.
Parallels: *Lachish III:* pl. 89:357; *Diban:* fig. 21:16, pl.
30:9; Amiran 1970: pl. 86:9, pl. 88:12 (Megiddo); *Beth
Shan:* fig. 70:15, fig. 10:13.

36. Oil Lamp

Lachish, Tomb 1002
Iron II C, 800–586 BCE
Clay: wheel-turned and fired
Ht. 3.8 cm., diam. 14.4 cm.
Archaeology Acquisition Fund   JM 12-73.46

Description: shallow bowl; wide, everted rim
forming flat ledge; pinched mouth; round base.
Orange-red ware; fire-blackened spout.
Bibliography: *Lachish III:* pl. 83:148.

37. Oil Lamp

Lachish, Tomb 106
Iron II C, 800–586 BCE
Clay: wheel-turned and fired
Ht. 5.2 cm., diam. 11.7 cm.
Archaeology Acquisition Fund   JM 12–73.54

The thick, clumsy base of this lamp is a feature
peculiar to southern Israel in the Iron II C Period,
and represents a new development in the
millennium-long tradition of round-based lamps.
Normally, a potter will trim the base of a vessel
to the desired shape, but in this instance the
potters apparently did not trim the clay matrix
created on the bottom of the bowl during the
throwing process.

Description: very shallow bowl with wide, everted
rim and pinched mouth; carination at attachment of
bowl to high disc base; thick walls. Orange ware and
core; fire-blackened spout; piece of rim missing.
Bibliography: *Lachish III:* pl. 83:153.
Parallels: Amiran 1970: pl. 100:20 (Beit Mirsim); *Beer-
sheba I:* pl. 56:5, pl. 63:135.

38

40

39

41

38. Female Pillar Figurine

Lachish, Tomb 106
Iron II A–C, 1000–586 BCE
Clay: hand-formed body, mold-formed head, fired
Ht. 15.5 cm., width 7.5 cm.
Archaeology Acquisition Fund   JM 12–73.268a

The function of these nude female pillar figurines, common throughout Iron Age Israel, is still being debated. They have been interpreted as either cultic objects, instruments of sympathetic magic, or toys (Holland 1977: 132–134). The general consensus appears to be that the pillar figurines probably represent some form of "mother goddess" personifying fertility, possibly the goddess Astarte of the Canaanites, Sidonians, and Philistines. A few examples of these or other "cult" figurines (such as model couches, birds, or rattles) have been found in sanctuaries in Israel. However, it seems doubtful that the figurines were publicly worshipped as idols. The frequency of their presence in homes and tombs suggests they may have served an amuletic or superstitious function, in this world and in the afterlife.

Description: solid cylindrical body; flared base conically indented; face poorly molded, features indistinct and abraded; two horizontal rows of curls across forehead, wig plain, head comes to rounded point; prominent breasts, arms bent with hands a little below breasts. Orange ware; reconstructed join of break at shoulder, and of missing portion of base.
Bibliography: *Lachish III:* pl. 27:4.
Parallels: Holland 1977: Type A.VIII, pp. 126–127 for full distribution of this type; *Lachish V:* pl. 12:1–3, *Beer-sheba I:* pl. 27:4–9.

39. Model of a Bed or Couch

Lachish, Tomb 1002
Iron II A–C, 1000–700 BCE
Clay: hand-molded and fired
Ht. 9.7 cm., length 11.7 cm., width 8.3 cm.
Archaeology Acquisition Fund   JM 12–73.450

Models of couches or divan beds have also, like the female figurines, been associated with rituals dedicated to Astarte. For example, the discovery of a figurine, couch, and miniature pedestaled lamp in a domestic room of Beer-sheba led the excavator to reconstruct the spot as an area of home cultic worship (*Beer-sheba I:* 17). Whatever their function, their shapes enable us to gain an idea of the appearance of Iron Age furniture, none of which has survived, probably because it was constructed of wood.

Description: narrow four-legged bed with back or headboard. Orange ware with straw impressions; corner of headboard missing.

Parallels: *Lachish III:* pl. 29:20–22; Holland 1977: 154, fig. 9:19,20 (Jerusalem); *Beer-sheba I:* pl. 27:3, pl. 28:5,6; *Gezer I:* pl. 36:3.

40. Bird Figurine

Lachish, Tomb 1002
Iron II A–C, 1000–700 BCE
Clay: hand-molded and fired
Ht. of back and wings 4.5 cm.
Archaeology Acquisition Fund   JM 12–73.268b

Those scholars who interpret these bird figurines as cult objects connect them with the symbol of Astarte, the dove (Holland 1977: 152). The Lachish Iron Age tombs have yielded several; none were found in a stratified level on the tell.

Description: bird with outstretched wings and pointed tail on solid pillar base. Mottled buff and orange ware; head and wingtips reconstructed, break in tail repaired.
Bibliography: *Lachish III:* 235, probably F.1290 or F.1301.
Parallels: *Lachish III:* pl. 28:12; Holland 1977: Type E.I, p. 152, fig. 8:10 (Jerusalem), pp. 126–127 for distribution in Israel.

41. Rattle

Lachish, Tomb 1002
Iron II A–C, 1000–586 BCE
Clay: wheel-turned, slipped, fired
Ht. 6.6 cm., length 8 cm.
Archaeology Acquisition Fund   JM 12–73.428

Hollow objects containing pebbles or clay pieces are found in numerous Iron Age sites, mainly in tombs (*Lachish III:* 376, Holland 1977: 154). An instrument that was shaken, possibly a rattle, is mentioned as being played during David's transport of the Ark to Jerusalem (II Sam. 6:5), thereby suggesting that the rattle shown here was a musical instrument of the Iron Age. Rattles are also found in the Late Bronze Age in association with cultic installations; this has probably led to their interpretation as cultic objects in the Iron Age (Paul and Dever 1974: 248). However, there is always the possibility that rattles were children's toys, just as they are today.

Description: concave-sided, hollow body, closed on either end with convex disc; hole of different size on either end. Orange ware; red slip; mottled gray surface.
Bibliography: *Lachish III:* 235, either F.1291, 1299 or 1300.
Parallels: *Lachish III:* pl. 27:6,9, pl. 28:15, p. 376; Holland 1977:154, fig. 9:16 (Jerusalem).

42

"Cypro-Phoenician" Ware

Two juglets in the collection are examples of a possibly imported type of pottery generally referred to as "Cypro-Phoenician" ware. The exact place of origin of this black-on-red ware has been widely debated and suggestions range from the coastal areas of Syria, Lebanon, or Israel to Cyprus (*Beer-sheba I:* 40; Amiran 1970: 286; *Lachish III:* 297–298).

"Cypro-Pheonician" ware is an excellent candidate for the kind of clay origin analysis now being performed on Mycenaean, Greek, Philistine, and other types of Cypriot pottery discovered in Israel (e.g., *Ashdod II-III:* 216–219). By analyzing the chemical composition of clay beds in areas believed to be the origin of an "import" and comparing it with the composition of the "imports," archaeologists are beginning to gain more conclusive means of identifying imports and a greater understanding of their distribution network.

If this ware was in fact imported into Israel, it is not clear exactly why: whether for its contents or for the sake of the vessel itself. It would therefore be of great interest to study the extent and nature of this alleged foreign commercial contact.

43

42. "Cypro-Phoenician" Juglet

Eastern Mediterranean
Iron II A–C, 1000–700 BCE
Clay: wheel-turned, rolled handle, slipped, painted, burnished, fired
Ht. 11.2 cm., diam. 7.5 cm.
Purchased in Jerusalem, 1969   JM 24–69

Description: globular body; tall, narrow neck flaring widely to rim, sharp horizontal ridge below midpoint; rim everted; handle attached below neck ridge to shoulder, oval cross-section; base flat. Orange ware; pink core; orange slip; black paint: one band on rim, three bands on neck, six narrow bands above body midpoint, one thick band below; three concentric circles of four rings each on shoulder; paint applied after wheel-burnishing.
Parallels: *Lachish III:* pl. 36:64, pl. 88:336,337; *Beer-sheba I:* pl. 45:14; *Beth Shan:* figs. 13:8, 18:22, 61:6.

43. "Cypro-Phoenician" Miniature Pitcher

Eastern Mediterranean
Iron II A–C, 1000–586 BCE
Clay: wheel-turned, pulled handle, slipped, burnished, painted, fired
Ht. 11.4 cm., diam. 8.2 cm.
Purchased in Jerusalem, 1969   JM 23–69

Description: globular body; narrow cylindrical neck with trefoil mouth; handle has oval cross-section; ring base. Red ware; red slip mottled with gray; black-painted decoration consists of six concentric circles on shoulder (two placed one above the other), and four large circles on lower body with small concentric circles in centers; horizontal bands on rim, neck, and near midpoint; painted handle.
Parallels: *Lachish III:* pl. 88:338; Amiran 1970: pl. 97:7 (Megiddo).

45

44

44. Miniature Bowl with Vertical Lug Handles

Lachish, Tomb 106
Iron II C, 800–586 BCE
Clay: hand-formed and fired
Ht. 3.1 cm., diam. 8.1 cm.
Archaeology Acquisition Fund   JM 12–73.120

The interior and rim of this bowl are quite fire-blackened; presumably it served either as a lamp or possibly an incense burner. Lamps are ubiquitous in tombs in Israel down into the Byzantine Period at least, but we cannot ascertain whether they were intended to light the way of the visitors or to accompany the deceased in the afterlife, or perhaps both. This bowl is a unique example of its type at Lachish, although a second similar miniature bowl of slightly different shape was also discovered in the same tomb.

Description: convex sides, gently carinated at midpoint; rim thickened and convex inside and out, rounded edge; base flat; four pinched vertical lug handles at rim, roughly equidistant. Pink ware; heavy fire-blackening on interior.
Bibliography: *Lachish III:* 274, pl. 81:107.
Parallels: *Lachish III:* pl. 102:106; Amiran 1970: photo 216 (for vertical lug handles).

45. Stamp Seal

Lachish (?)
Iron II A–C, 1000–586 BCE
Limestone: carved and drilled
Ht. 1.4 cm., diam. 1.4 cm.
Provenance lost
Archaeology Acquisition Fund   JM 12–73.413

Seals were used in the ancient Near East to denote personal ownership. In regions where papyrus and ink were the principal writing materials, the papyri would have been rolled and tied with string. A ball of clay (*bulla*) would have been placed over the knot, and the seal impressed into the clay, thereby signifying ownership. A jar of such *bullae* was discovered at Lachish in a possible storage area (*Lachish V:* 19–22, pls. 20,21). The impressions mainly consisted of personal names, but two examples of figural decoration (rosettes) were also found among the cache. The seventeen *bullae*, taken from the sealed papyri, may have been kept for record purposes.

This seal, although its provenance has been lost, is very likely from Lachish. It is nearly identical in size, material, and decoration to a surface find from Lachish, illustrated in *Lachish III* (pl. 45:148, p. 372). The only difference between them is the absence of a horizontal extension of the animal's hind foot in the drawing, which could have been overlooked by the artist or have been scratched recently into the soft stone. Since the Jewish Museum seal was part of the Colt Collection and the drawn seal is published as belonging to Colt, it seems likely that they are the same seal.

Description: conoid seal with horizontal drill hole; seal depicts a horned quadruped, possibly a deer or antelope. Buff, gray-brown surface.
Parallels: *Lachish III:* pl. 45:147.

46

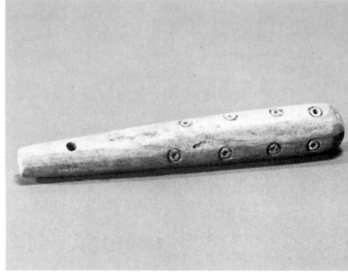

47

46. Spindle Whorl

Lachish, Tomb 106
Iron II C, 800–586 BCE
Steatite: incised and drilled
Ht. 1.7 cm., diam. 2.2 cm.
Archaeology Acquisition Fund   U 7530

In the making of thread, fibers are wound onto a spindle; whorls are placed on the spindle in order to provide it with more spinning momentum. The discovery at Megiddo of a Late Bronze Age bone spindle with two hemispherical whorls still in place has aided in the interpretation of these objects (*Megiddo I:* pl. 95:38).

It is perhaps surprising that only five of these utilitarian items came from houses of Iron Age Lachish. Their burial with the deceased suggests either the inclusion of a favorite everyday object or occupational tool, or the wish for the continuation of earthly activities in the afterlife.

Description: hemisphere; two incised horizontal bands near flat base; vertical drill hole.
Bibliography: *Lachish III:* pl. 54:42.
Parallels: *Lachish V:* pl. 16:3,4, pl. 34:5,9; *Megiddo I:* pl. 95:20,36; *Samaria-Sebaste III:* fig. 92a:13.

47. Netting Bobbin

Israel
Iron II B–C, 900–586 BCE
Bone: carved, punched, drilled
Length 7.2 cm., diam. 1 cm.
Purchased in Israel
Gift of the Betty and Max Ratner Collection   1981–220

Bone objects with center-dot decoration were frequent finds in the Iron Age tombs at Lachish and in many sites in Israel. Originally called pendants, archaeologists now interpret them as netting bobbins. The thread would have passed through the perforation and been wound around the bobbin. The net weaver would then use the bobbin as a needle, unwinding the thread as he or she wove. Since these bone bobbins were distributed in both coastal and inland sites, the nets they were used to produce might have been intended for fowling as well as fishing.

Description: long, truncated conical form; perforation near top; decorated with four vertical rows of four center-dot circles.
Bibliography: Kozloff 1978: no. RC 178, fig. 36.
Parallels: *Lachish III:* pl. 56:14, pl. 55:23,45,46, pl. 54:76; *Megiddo I:* pl. 97:8,9,16.

48. "Lotus-seed" Bead Necklace

Probably Israel
Late Bronze Age II B–Iron Age II A–C, 1300–586 BCE
Carnelian: carved and drilled
Length ca. 48.5 cm., max. bead length 2.3 cm.
Purchased in Israel, said to be from a tomb near Gaza
Gift of the Betty and Max Ratner Collection
  1981–158

Scholars long ago likened the shape of these beads to lotus seeds, although today they are called "bottle-shaped" as well. The form appears to have enjoyed a long period of popularity, for it has been found in Late Bronze Age through Iron Age contexts, including the Lachish tombs. This longevity indicates either the status of the beads as heirlooms or their continuous production. Whatever the explanation, they demonstrate the continuity between the Canaanite and Israelite cultures. The "lotus-seed" bead has a wide distribution in Israel, Egypt, and Cyprus (Tadmor and Misch-Brandl 1980: 76).

Description: 22 lotus-shaped beads and one larger central one, separated by four short, barrel-shaped beads; 17 short biconical beads spaced with short barrels at the ends.
Bibliography: Kozloff 1978: no. RC 116, color pl. 4.
Parallels: Tadmor and Misch-Brandl 1980:76; *Lachish III:* pl. 38, pl. 67:144,145, pl. 66:47; *Megiddo I:* pl. 90:7, 20,48.

49

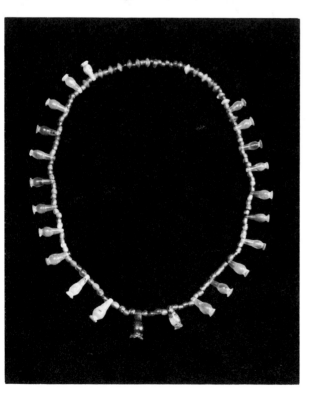

48

49. Necklace

Lachish, Tomb 1002
Iron Age II C, 800–586 BCE
Carnelian: carved and drilled
Length 40.3 cm., max. bead length 2.3 cm.
Archaeology Acquisition Fund   JM 12–73.451

Description: necklace made of long biconical beads (5), short biconicals (9), long barrels (7), short barrels (33), short oblates (13), large short biconical beads (2), and 4 rectangular spacers with two lateral drill holes and central groove. Stringed arrangement is modern since beads not found *in situ*, but when tomb fill was sieved (*Lachish III:* 236).
Bibliography: *Lachish III:* pl. 67:112, pl. 66:5,14, 17,23,24,44,55.
Parallels: *Lachish V:* pl. 16:13,15,19.

50. Earring (NOT ILLUSTRATED)

Lachish, Tomb 106
Iron II C, 800–586 BCE
Silver: cast
Length 2.4 cm.
Archaeology Acquisition Fund   JM 12–73.392

Description: incomplete ring with ball drop; upper part of ring thinner than lower.
Bibliography: *Lachish III:* pl. 54:4.
Parallels: *Megiddo I:* pl. 86:21.

51. Bangle, possibly a Bracelet

Lachish, Tomb 116
Iron II B–C, 900–586 BCE
Bronze: cast and hammered
Diam. 8.7 cm., diam. of cross-section 0.9 cm.
Archaeology Acquisition Fund   JM 12–73.433

This thinner bangle may have been worn as a bracelet, since two thinner rings were found *in situ* on the arms of two skeletons at Lachish.

Description: round cross-section with flattened bottom; ends flat, do not quite meet.
Bibliography: *Lachish III:* pl. 55:3.
Parallels: *Lachish V:* 76, pl. 36:19.

52. Bangle, probably an Anklet

Lachish, Tomb 116
Iron II B–C, 900–586 BCE
Bronze: cast and hammered
Diam. 10.2 cm., diam. of cross-section 1.8 cm., wt. 431.3 gms.
Archaeology Acquisition Fund   JM 12–73.429

At Lachish, these thick rings come exclusively from Iron Age tombs where several undisturbed cave burials still had the rings in place above the ankle (e.g., *Lachish III:* pl. 9:3). There are not enough published intact burials to determine whether the anklets were limited to a particular age, sex, or social status. They have most recently been interpreted as a means of exchange in Israel before the introduction of coinage from Persia in the 5th century BCE (see no. 59).

Description: round cross-section with flat ends that do not quite meet.
Bibliography: *Lachish III:* pl. 55:2.

51

52

Stamped Jar Handles

For the past century, archaeologists at Iron Age sites in Israel have been discovering the handles of large storage jars that were stamped with seals before firing. Very few of the complete, stamped jars have survived until today, probably because the early excavators of Israel were not interested in saving pottery fragments, but kept only the handles. The contexts of the stamped jar handles, and presumably the jars they belonged to, are almost exclusively dwelling units.

The images on seal impressions break down into two main types. The first, called royal seals, bear the inscription in ancient Hebrew: "[Belonging] to the king," placed above either a four-winged scarab or a two-winged sundisc. Below the figure is inscribed one of four possible place names: Hebron, Ziph, Socoh, or the unidentified *Mmšt*. The second type of seal bears only an inscribed name and is called a private seal, although today scholars interpret it as that of a royal official.

The stamped storage jars, found in sites all over southern Israel and associated with the king and his officials, would seem to pertain in some way to governmental economic administration. Yet scholars have been debating their significance for the past century and have come to no conclusive interpretation of their function (Welten 1969: 118–142). In the case of the royal seals, four main theories have been advanced: (1) they were meant to be filled with agricultural products by the populace to be sent as taxes to the king; (2) they were produced by private potters, working in the four above-named cities, who undertook royal commissions for storage jars; (3) the four places named represent the administrative seats of royal estates, and the jars contained the oil and wine produced there; (4) the royal stamp guaranteed the standardized capacity of the vessel. This last suggestion has now been possibly disproven, since the capacity of six complete jars with stamped handles have been measured and found to have a wide range in volume (Ussishkin 1978: 76–81). Perhaps only with the excavation of the four sites named in the seal impressions can we understand the function of the royal stamped storage jars.

In the case of the so-called private stamps, scholars now agree that they too are associated with royal business, based on a recent discovery of two complete jars at Lachish, each with four handles impressed with both royal and "private" stamps (Ussishkin 1976: 1). The fact that handles with the same official's stamp have been found at more than one site may also imply centralized production or distribution centers.

53

53. Jar Handle with Royal Seal Impression

Lachish, surface find
Iron II C, late 8th cent. BCE
Clay: body fragment wheel-turned, handle pulled and impressed, fired
Width of body fragment 7.4 cm., width of handle 5 cm.; ht. of impression 3.5 cm., width 2.2 cm.
Archaeology Acquisition Fund   JM 12–73.278

Inscription in ancient Hebrew:
Lmlkh Hbrn
[Belonging] to the King/Hebron.

Description: handle with one or two vertical ridges on upper surface and single ridge on lower. Oval seal impression is upside down; upper line of inscription *lmlkh* poorly impressed; four-winged scarab with :h upper left wing abraded; *Hbrn* clearly stamped below.
Bibliography: unpublished.
Parallels: Diringer 1941: pl. VI:11 (Class II); *Lachish III:* pl. 46A:11; Welten 1969: Type HI B1.

54. Jar Handle with Royal Seal Impression

Lachish, grid square K.14/J.14, depth 271.6 m. ASL
Iron II C, late 8th cent. BCE
Clay: jar wheel-turned, pulled handle, impressed, fired
Length of body fragment 11.7 cm., max. width of
handle 5 cm.; ht. of impression 2.1 cm., width of seal
impression 3.1 cm.
Archaeology Acquisition Fund   JM 12–73.272

Inscription in ancient Hebrew:
[Lmlkh]/Hbrn
[Belonging to the king]/Hebron.

Description: handle has double, vertical ridges and
oval cross-section; seal not completely impressed;
inscription below two-winged disc. Reddish ware.
Bibliography: Diringer 1941: 93, pl. VII:6 (Class III);
Lachish III: 342, pl. 46B:6.
Parallels: Welten 1969: Type HII B1.

54

55. Jar Handle with Official's Stamp Impression

Lachish, grid square K.14/J.14, depth 271.6 m. ASL
Iron II C, late 8th–7th cent. BCE
Clay: pulled handle, impressed, fired
Handle width 3.6 cm.; seal impression (preserved
portion) length 0.8 cm., width 0.65 cm.
Archaeology Acquisition Fund   JM 12–73.286

Inscription in ancient Hebrew:
Lšbn/' Š[hr]
Belonging to Shebna [son of] Šh[ahar].

The reading of the name on this partially
stamped seal is facilitated by comparison with
three well-stamped impressions of the same
official's seal found at Tell en-Nasbeh.

Description: small fragment of jar body; handle has
oval cross-section with two vertical ridges; seal
impression is incomplete on left side; inscription of
official's name on two lines; a single line borders seal
face with two horizontal lines in center; seal impressed
diagonally. Pink ware; dark gray core.
Bibliography: Diringer 1941: 46, pl. IV:1; *Lachish III:*
341–2, pl. 47B:1.
Parallels: Hestrin and Dayagi-Mendels 1980: no. 19.

56. Jar Handle with Official's Stamp Impression

Lachish, grid square K.15, 270.7 m. ASL
Iron II C, late 8th cent. BCE
Clay: pulled handle, impressed, fired
Width of handle 4.6 cm.; length of seal impression
1.2 cm., ht. 1.1 cm.
Archaeology Acquisition Fund   JM 12–73.280

Inscription in ancient Hebrew:
Mšlm 'hmlkh
Meshullam [son of] Ahimelekh .

Nine seal impressions of Meshullam (son of)
Ahimelekh, excavated at Lachish, have been
published. This previously unpublished specimen
makes the tenth.

Description: small fragment of jar body; fragment of
handle is flat with oval cross-section and one vertical
ridge preserved; stamp is oval and impressed upside-
down; name of official in two lines separated by
double line; single line around seal border. Orange ware.
Bibliography: unpublished.
Parallels: Diringer 1941: 41, pl. III:4–6; *Lachish III:*
341, pl. 47A:4–6; Hestrin and Dayagi-Mendels 1979: no.
14; Ussishkin 1978: 76–77.

55

56

The Iron Age Weight System

It is uncertain whether the ancient Israelites used a system of weights and measures that was standardized and regulated by the state (de Vaux 1961: 195–196). However, in the case of stone weights, there is a suggestion in the Bible of an official or national standard. The basic unit of weight in ancient Israel was the shekel. The commodity to be bought or sold would have been weighed in a balance scale against the standardized shekel weights, each marked with their value. The commodity could then be exchanged for other desired products of the same value, or possibly for bronze rings like no. 59.

Numerous passages in the Bible reckon shekel weights after the "shekel of the sanctuary" (Ex. 30:13), while other passages refer to the king's weight (2 Sam. 14:26) and the merchant's weight (Gen. 23:16). These quotes suggest that while different approximate standards may have existed, one could always refer to the royal or priestly weight for an absolute standard. However, there are no commandments in the Bible exhorting the use of any particular standard; only that the weights be just and that no attempt be made to cheat in weighing by having "diverse weights, a great and a small" (Lev. 19:35–36).

A recent attempt to study the value of the weights by region has led to the conclusion that the Judean shekel averages 11.4 gms. (Meshorer 1978: 131). Other weights in the series represent various sixths of the shekel; the smallest weights, marked with two vertical strokes, average at two-sixths of a shekel (3.8 gms.); the *beqa* at one-half a shekel (5.7 gms.); the *pim* at two-thirds of a shekel (7.6 gms.); and the *netzef* at five-sixths of a shekel.

57

57. *Netzef* Weight

Israel
Iron II C, 800–586 BCE
Limestone: carved and incised
Diam. 2 cm., ht. 1.8 cm., wt. 10 gms.
Purchased in Israel
Gift of the Betty and Max Ratner Collection   1981–124
Inscription in ancient Hebrew:
  Nṣp (*Netzef*)

Netzef weights, because of their lack of mention in the Bible, unusual shape, and citation in the Ugaritic system of Syria, had long been thought to be from another weight system, although they were frequently found in Israel. However, the average Judean *netzef* weight of 9.5 grams comes to five-sixths of a Judean shekel, suggesting that the *netzef* was an integral part of the local weight system.

Description: dome with narrow, flat bottom, incised inscription on top of dome. Pink limestone, one circle of tan color.
Bibliography: Kozloff 1978: no. RC 82, fig. 34.
Parallels: *Lachish III:* pl. 50:7.

58

58. *Beqa* Weight

Israel
Iron II C, 7th–6th cent. BCE
Limestone: carved and incised
Diam. 1.9 cm., ht. 1.2 cm., wt. 6.1 gms.
Purchased in Israel
Gift of Joy Ungerleider, 1968   JM 232–68a

Inscription in ancient Hebrew:
  Bq' (Beqa)

Description: dome shape with flat bottom and
incised inscription on top of dome. Mottled buff to
pink stone.
Parallels: *Lachish III:* 351:38,40,42.

59. **Bangle** (NOT ILLUSTRATED)

Lachish, Tomb 116
Iron A–C, 1000–586 BCE
Bronze: cast and hammered
Diam. 10.1 cm., diam. of cross-section 1.7 cm., wt.
  362.15 gms.
Archaeology Acquisition Fund   JM 12–73.431

Archaeologists have recently suggested that these
bangles, formerly considered as items of jewelry
(e.g., no. 51), may also have functioned as an
exchange medium (Dayton 1974); Meshorer; 1978
129). This hypothesis is based on a study of their
weights, and on the possibility that they were
gradated and standardized. The unmarked
bangles would have been weighed at the time of
sale to determine their value.

Description: round cross-section with flat bottom,
flat ends with slight gap between them.
Bibliography: *Lachish III:* pl. 55:2.

60. **Sling Shot (?)** (NOT ILLUSTRATED)

Tell Ajjul, context unknown
Date undetermined
Clay: hand-formed and baked
Diam. 4.6 cm.
Archaeology Acquisition Fund   JM 12–73.270

Sling shots were the weapons used by shepherds,
as in the story of David and Goliath. However,
they were also potent weapons of war used by
crack slingers who "could sling a stone at a hair
and would not miss" (Judg. 20:16). The sling was
made of a leather thong that was wide at the
center (de Vaux 1961: 244), and the shot was
generally a round pebble or a specially formed
stone. It is conceivable that this object in the
Jewish Museum collection, although made of
mud, was also used as a sling shot. Masses of
stone shots were found at Lachish in an area
inside the city wall, which has recently been
interpreted as the Assyrian siege ramp of 701 BCE
(Ussishkin 1978: 68; *Lachish III:* 55).

Description: smooth surface, irregular round form.
Buff clay.
Parallels: *Lachish III:* pl. 40:5 (stone examples).

61

61. Trilobe Arrowhead

Probably Israel
Iron Age II C–Persian Period, 7th–4th cent. BCE
Bronze: cast
Length 3.9 cm., width 0.9 cm.
Purchased in Israel
Gift of the Betty and Max Ratner Collection   1981–133

Trilobe arrowheads were a standard missile of
the Persian army, and their use in the Levant
probably diffused from Iran (*Lachish V:* 80). Two
unstratified arrowheads of this type were found
at Lachish, both of bronze. It has been suggested
that the use of bronze made the mass production
of these weapons possible, because they could be
cast quickly in molds rather than hand-wrought,
as is necessary for iron products (cf. no. 62).

Description: round socket, round body with three
sharp blades or lobes; tip blunt, probably broken.
Bibliography: Kozloff 1978: no. RC 91, fig. 24.
Parallels: *Lachish V:* pl. 36:15; *Lachish III:* 386, pl.
60:53.

62. Trilobe Arrowhead (NOT ILLUSTRATED)

Probably Israel
Iron II–Persian Period, 7th–4th cent. BCE
Iron: wrought
Length 4.7 cm., width 1.4 cm.
Purchased in Israel, 1981
Gift of the Betty and Max Ratner Collection   1982–9

Description: round socket, round body, three blades
or lobes, sharp tip.

63. Spearhead

Israel
Iron II A–C, 1000–586 BCE
Iron: wrought
Length 21.6 cm., width 3.2 cm.
Purchased in Israel
Gift of the Betty and Max Ratner Collection   1981–96

Description: oval-shaped blade with midrib from
socket to tip; socket with circular cross-section.
Bibliography: Kozloff 1978: no. RC 54, fig. 23 right.
Parallels: *Lachish III:* pl. 56:30.

64. Plough Point

Israel
Iron I-II, 1200–586 BCE
Iron: wrought
Length 26.5 cm., diam. of socket 3.3 cm.
Purchased in Israel
Gift of the Betty and Max Ratner Collection   1981–97

A number of iron plough points have been
excavated at sites in Israel, several from Lachish.
They were meant to fit over a wooden
ploughshare, and the flanged sides would have
been hammered together to form a close-fitting
socket (*Lachish V:* 81).

Description: point has roughly square cross-section,
socket is round.
Bibliography: Kozloff 1978: no. RC 55, fig. 23.
Parallels: *Lachish V:* 77, pl. 37:14; *Lachish III:* pl.
61:1,3; *Beer-sheba I:* 43–46.

65. Adze Head

Israel
Iron Age (?), 1200–586 BCE
Iron: wrought
Length 17 cm., width 7 cm., ht. 4.5 cm.
Provenance unknown
Archaeology Acquisition Fund   JM 12–73.366

Description: flat, wide blade, widest at socket and
narrowing toward the square-ended scraping edge,
which is partially eroded; butt of the adze is high and
rectangular in form; circular hole for the vertical shaft
or handle set at an angle, with raised ridge around the
hole on bottom.
Parallels: *Megiddo I:* pl. 83:18,19; *Lachish V:* pl. 38:3
(for chisels of similar form).

63—

64

65

66

66. Pickax

Israel
Iron Age II C-Hellenistic Period, 7th–1st cent. BCE
Iron: cast and hammered
Length 22.6 cm., ht. of ax blade 4.6 cm., width at
    socket 3.6 cm.
Purchased in Israel, 1981
Gift of the Betty and Max Ratner Collection   1982–8

Description: ax blade has parallel sides and curved
cutting edge, wedge-shaped in top view (wide shaft
area narrows to point at cutting edge); pick is
rectangular in cross-section, widest at shaft area and
all facets narrowing to point, circular vertical shaft
hole.
Parallels: Hennessy 1970: pl. XIB (Samaria Sebaste);
Weinberg 1969: 22 (Tell Anafa); *Samaria-Sebaste III:* fig.
113:8.

The conquest of Judah by the Babylonians and the subsequent Exile were watershed events in the history of ancient Israel. With the razing of the Temple and the exile of the leaders of the Judean community both the religious and political bases of Jewish life were shattered. Without the Temple to serve as the focal point of the culture, it is probable that the Torah increasingly became the spiritual center of the religion in Babylon, perhaps compiled for public readings and study as a substitute for Temple sacrifice. Under the guidance of the Exilic prophets, most notably Ezekiel, Jerusalem continued to be the symbol of the national identity and for the hope that the Jews would return to Israel to rebuild the Temple.

67. Inscribed Cylinder of Nebuchadnezzar II

Marad, Temple (Babylonia)
Neo-Babylonian Period, 604–562 BCE
Clay: inscribed and fired
Ht. 22.6 cm., diam. 13.4 cm.
Loaned by the Yale Babylonian Collection   NCBT 2314

This cylinder, written in Neo-Babylonian script, commemorates the construction of a temple in the city of Marad by Nebuchadnezzar II. This is the same king whose armies destroyed the cities of Judah in 587/6 BCE and exiled many of its inhabitants to Babylon. The cylinder was buried in a foundation box in the temple and was meant to be read by future kings when they renovated or rebuilt it.

Description: truncated conical form, hollow, with each end partially closed; cuneiform inscription in three columns; top end somewhat convex, bottom flat.
Parallels: *Yale Oriental Series IX*: 36–37; Berger 1973: 277–284.

67

Excavation
the Jewish Quarter
Jerusale

Photograph Above
Top left: no. 81; Bottom left; no. 80;
Center: no. 101; Top right: no. 102;
Bottom right: no. 100.

Photograph Right
Front row: no. 93; no. 97; no. 98; no. 96;
no. 94; Back row: no. 95, no. 89, no. 90.

Following Page
Front row: no. 88, no. 108, no. 92,
no. 87; Back row: no. 86, no. 118.

Aspects of the State, the Home, and Religion

Introduction: Historical Background and Jerusalem

In 539 BCE., Cyrus, King of Persia, issued a proclamation that allowed the Jews who had been exiled to Babylonia to return to Israel. Although only a small percentage of the Jews returned, the Temple in Jerusalem was rebuilt between 519 and 515 BCE, on a scale much more modest than the Temple that Solomon had constructed in the tenth century BCE. Thus begins, in both archaeological and historical terminology, the Second Temple Period, which lasted for almost six centuries, until the Romans sacked and razed the Temple and Jerusalem in 70 CE.

The events of the period from 515 BCE to 70 CE reflect Israel's unique geographical location as a crossroads between Egypt and Mesopotamia and, with the rise of the Aegean powers, between East and West. For two millennia the political status of the Levant had been controlled by the waxing and waning of the superpowers of the time, with Israel able to exert local autonomy only during a hiatus in the domination by foreign empires. Thus the Second Temple Period is subdivided into periods that are based on the shifting political control of the region: 536 to 330 BCE is the Persian Period; 330 to 164 BCE is the Hellenistic Period; 164 to 63 BCE is the Hasmonean Period; and 63 BCE to 70 CE is the Early Roman or Herodian Period.

When Alexander the Great's Macedonian army burst into the Near East in 332 BCE, it overwhelmed the Persian forces and subsequently annexed the whole of the Persian empire. For Alexander, Israel was little more than a passageway between Asia Minor and the splendors of Egypt. Only token resistance was offered at Gaza, with the rest of the region submitting to this newest of overlords.

Alexander's empire, however, was short-lived. Nine years after marching through the Levant he died of fever in Persia, and his whole kingdom was thereby plunged into a chaotic and sometimes frenetic power struggle between his subordinates. The Near East was divided between two of his generals, Seleucis in Mesopotamia and Syria, and Ptolemy in Egypt. Judea was at first under the aegis of the Ptolemies, but the Seleucids wrested control of the region from them in 198 BCE.

Both the Seleucid and Ptolemaic control over Judea intensified the spread of Hellenism (Greek culture) that had begun on a grand scale with Alexander. Jews in Jerusalem and, to a lesser extent, in the surrounding environs, were swept into the strong stream of Greek thought, styles in dress, art, architecture, and language. One of the impacts of Hellenism was to cause a rift in the Jewish community between the Hellenized aristocracy, who were the class in society most affected by the emerging cosmopolitan nature of Jerusalem, and that segment of the population that clung to past traditions and rejected Hellenization as apostasy.

When civil disorders between the Hellenized Jews and the more traditional Jews wracked Jerusalem, the holy city was occupied by the Seleucid army. Seeking to stifle further insurrection by forcing the Jews to assimilate, the Seleucids abandoned their policy of religious toleration and converted the Temple into a shrine to Zeus, thereby enraging the Jewish population. Finally, in 164 BCE, the Jews revolted and, under the leadership of Judah Maccabee (of the Hasmonean family), they re-established an independent Jewish state. Under the guidance of Judah's brothers Simon and

Jonathan, the kingdom was extended almost to the borders of the empire Solomon had created eight hundred years earlier.

For almost a century, the new state prospered during the decline of the Hellenistic kingdoms in Syria and Egypt, during internecine Greek conflicts and before Roman interest turned to the lands east of the Mediterranean.

However, the inevitable expansion of Rome soon engulfed Judea, and in 63 BCE Pompey's troops took Jerusalem. Herod was installed as ruler of the new Roman district soon thereafter (37 BCE). The Early Roman period was one of contrast for the Jews: the Temple was rebuilt and beautified as never before and the capital expanded and modernized However, the slow accretion of religious and political restrictions finally pushed the Jewish population into rebellion in 66 CE. At first the insurgents were successful and gained control of Jerusalem for three years. This brief gasp of independence was snuffed out by the Roman armies in the year 70 CE, when they razed the city and plundered the Temple treasures.

Excavations of the city of Jerusalem reflect the historical fortunes of the local population from the time of the return from Exile (539) until the destruction of the Temple in 70 CE. Since 1864, over fifty different expeditions have concentrated their efforts in the Old City, ranging from brief clearings and investigations of small areas to the major excavation of the Jewish Quarter of the Old City begun in 1969 and the ongoing exploration of the City of David to the south of the Temple Mount. Most of these excavations have been limited by the continued occupation of the city in areas overlying important sections of the ancient city. For example, sealed beneath the inviolable Temple Mount are the remains of the Second Temple and Herod's Palace, and residential portions of the Hasmonean and Herodian cities are buried beneath modern homes and markets. Excavations have had to work around these occupied areas and be careful not to undermine existing structures. Thus, an overview of Jerusalem from Second Temple times is often difficult, and archaeologists are frequently forced to generalize about the city's composition and extent from relatively small amounts of data. This, in turn, has led to greater dependence upon ancient historical sources to supplement our archaeological knowledge. Toward this end, the most important of the ancient records are the writings of the Roman Jewish historian Josephus; the "Intertestamental" literature known as the Apocrypha; the New Testament; and the Mishnah and Talmud.

Jerusalem is built on and between a series of valleys and inclines, a topography that governed the building efforts of kings from David to Herod. Bisecting the city on a north-south line, the Tyropoeon Valley separates the Temple Mount on the east from the western "Upper City" (present day Jewish Quarter). Just south of the Temple Mount, also to the east of the Tyropoeon, is the City of David.

The discovery of a clearly stratified Persian Period level in the City of David is the first glimpse archaeologists have had into the city of the sixth to fourth century BCE. Sandwiched between the lower Iron Age destruction level and base of the later Hellenistic fortifications was found a distinct occupation level containing Persian pottery and jar handles stamped "Yehud," the name of the Persian sub-province. The lack of such evidence from the Upper City suggests that Persian occupation was limited to the southernmost spur of the city.

Apparently, the city of early Hellenistic times did not expand far beyond the borders of the previous Persian city. Rhodian amphora handles (see nos. 70, 71) were found in a late fourth or third century BCE context in the City of David; few have been found in such contexts around the Temple Mount or in the Upper City (Jewish Quarter excavations). The establishment of the Hasmonean capital in Jerusalem in the second to first century BCE resulted in the first large expansion of the city since the Iron Age. Excavations in the Jewish Quarter have revealed evidence of Hasmonean buildings directly above Israelite remains, signaling the break in occupation in that part of the city during the Persian and Hellenistic Periods.

The final and most extensive expansion of Jerusalem occurred during the reign of the Roman-appointed king Herod the Great. Herod, in the tradition of Solomon, expended enormous energies to fortify and beautify the city. Evidence for his projects is found in almost every excavation in the Old City, ranging from the densely-settled City of David to the western and northern sections of the city.

The city destroyed by the Romans in 70 CE had reached its apogee: the Herodian Temple had been completed and the city had continued to develop as an economic center with a large aristocratic class, and trade networks that extended throughout the Mediterranean world. Ancient Jerusalem never recovered from the ravages of the Roman army, existing primarily as a site of pilgramage and the focus of Jewish identity.

The State (Nos. 68–82)

The political administration of Judah during the Second Temple Period may be divided into three broad phases. The first is comprised of semi-autonomous rule inaugurated under the Persians and continued during the early Hellenistic Period; the second is the independent Hasmonean state; and the third is the Roman rule of Palestine that began in 63 BCE.

The first sixty years of the Second Temple Period are among the most obscure in all of Jewish history. The Bible is almost completely silent about the events in Judea

under Persian rule from 515–458 BCE. From what can be gleaned from historical sources, the Persian governing policy allowed the Judean province to regulate many of its own domestic affairs under scrutiny from afar of the Persian court. This included maintenance of the Temple with religious matters under the control of the high priest.

Although the archaeological evidence is scant, it seems also to indicate that Judea may have maintained partial control of the country's administration and economy. Excavations in various sites of this period have yielded silver coins that date to the fourth century BCE. These coins are generally believed to have been manufactured locally; many bear the inscription "Yehud," the name of the Persian province. In addition, stamped jar handles with the word "Yehud" or "Yerushalem" are found on sites throughout Judea. Both of these pieces of evidence signify that the Judean government was semi-autonomous, minting their own coins and manufacturing specially stamped storage jars for the collection of taxes. It is possible, although by no means certain, that coinage and taxation were under the auspices of those in the employ of the Jerusalem Temple—a condition that would reflect the merger of the political and religious administrative functions of the community.

It appears that Judea remained semiautonomous during the brief time when it was part of Alexander's empire and during the subsequent hegemony of both the Ptolemies and the Seleucids. The continuity of the status quo is evidenced by the contents of two letters written during the third century BCE from Tobiah of Ammon (a region on the eastern side of the Jordan River) to the Ptolemies in Egypt. The Tobiad family had been appointed to govern Ammon during the Persian period; the letters indicate that they continued in this role during the Hellenistic period. This, too, may have been the case in Judea, for there is no evidence to suggest that the local Judean administration was replaced by either the Ptolemies or the Seleucids. Apparently, autonomy in domestic affairs was left in the hands of the high priest and a Council of Elders. Of course, court intrigue and local politics necessitated the intervention of the occupying powers to protect their own interests, but this seems to have been only sporadic and without lasting effect until the riots in Jerusalem.

The second phase of political administration is the emergence of the Hasmonean state in the middle of the second century BCE. Political independence, however, was not won with a single, decisive stroke. Rather, it was the result of a series of events that allowed the Hasmoneans to slowly sever the relationship between Judea and the Seleucids in Syria. The first blow was struck in 164 BCE when the Maccabees revolted successfully and were granted a degree of religious freedom. While they were able to rededicate the Temple in Jerusalem, a Syrian garrison (the Acra) was maintained on or near the Temple Mount and the province remained under the hegemony of the Seleucids.

It was not until 142 BCE that the next step toward political independence was achieved. Under the guidance of Judah Maccabee's brother Simon, Judea was freed from having to pay tribute to the Syrians and evicted the Syrian troops from the Acra in Jerusalem; Simon razed the Acra and established the Temple as the central point in the city.

Although Simon was able to extend the boundaries of the kingdom to the borders of the Davidic kingdom, most of the territory was lost when his son, John Hyrcanus, was defeated in a battle against the Syrians. It was not until 129 BCE that the course of international events favored the true emergence of Judea as an autonomous state. In that year Antiochus Sidetes, the king of Syria, fell in battle, and, in classic Near Eastern tradition, his kingdom began to dissipate under the civil strife caused by the competition among his generals for control of the kingdom. Freed from the yoke of the Syrians, John Hyrcanus was able to regain control of much of Judea and of Samaria to the north.

Unfortunately, historical sources give no details about the operations of the Hasmonean state, in terms of the administrative hierarchy in Jerusalem, the economic flow of goods or of international relations. Archaeological evidence is severely limited by the piecemeal excavations in Jerusalem, the Hasmonean capital since the time of Judah Maccabee. Although the picture of Hasmonean Jerusalem is far from comprehensive, excavations have shed light on the size of the city, the extent of its public building projects and on isolated aspects of economic administration and private commerce.

The primary symbol of the independence of the Hasmonean state was the minting of coins. Throughout the Mediterranean world, the issuing of coins was a symbol of autonomy that accompanied the emergence of even single cities following a period of subjugation. The first of the Hasmonean kings to issue a coin was Alexander Jannaeus. Coins were issued then by many of his successors and even during the three years (66–69) that the Jews achieved a modicum of independence during the Jewish Revolt.

The extent of the empire of John Hyrcanus I can be traced more by the destruction levels resulting from his conquest of cities throughout the Levant than by building projects or resettlements. Thus, destruction levels dated to his time have been uncovered at Samaria, Shechem and, from the time of Alexander Jannaeus, at Caeserea and Tell Anafa. Unfortunately, there is insufficient historical or archaeological evidence to reconstruct the role of the Hasmonean central government vis à vis local administration in the regulation of trade.

The major feature of Hasmonean

fortifications revealed in excavations around the Old City is a massive city wall referred to as the "First Wall" in the writings of Josephus. The Hasmonean wall was constructed of large stones that were uncarved and only roughly squared; they are easily distinguished from Herodian walls which were constructed of finely chiselled and embossed ashlars. Parts of the Hasmonean wall have been revealed in various sections of the city, including the eastern part (City of David), the western part (the Upper City, presently the Jewish Quarter) and in the courtyard of the Citadel. Thus, it appears that the Hasmonean city wall enclosed both the Upper and the Lower cities and connected to the Temple Mount.

The construction of the fortifications of the Hasmonean city would have necessitated a great deal of labor and financing. How this project was organized and supervised is not known, for there is no extant record of the Hasmonean machinery of state to compare to that recorded in the Bible about the reigns of David and Solomon. It is possible that the resources of the Temple treasury were used for these public building projects, resources that resulted from the Temple tax imposed on Jews living in Judea and surrounding countries. Additional revenues would have been generated during the three pilgrim festivals. The city would be mobbed with thousands of visitors, each of whom was bound by Jewish law to spend one-tenth of his yearly earnings in the Holy City (this was the so-called second tithe).

With the flow of people and goods into Jerusalem came an increasingly potent flood of Hellenistic culture. Excavations have unearthed great quantities of stamped jar handles of wine amphorae imported from Rhodes. New styles of pottery, jewelry and statuary were also imported from the west, replacing many of the indigenous forms that had been present for centuries. New industries, undoubtedly spurred by western contacts, blossomed in the city. In the Jewish Quarter, the excavators recovered a heap of glass refuse, including partially worked pieces and slag in the fill of an abandoned bath. Found together in the reservoir were remains of both blown glass and glass that has been produced by the use of a mold (see nos. 88–97). This was the first discovery of these two types of glass manufacturing found together in a well-stratified context able to be dated with some certainty. Based on the finding of coins of Alexander Jannaeus in association with the glass, it appears that glass blowing in Jerusalem began no later than the middle of the first century BCE. Unfortunately, the factory that had produced the glass fragments was not located.

In the political and religious administration of the Hasmonean state, the interaction—indeed, the confrontation—between Judaism and Hellenism came to the fore. To a certain extent the maintenance of religion impinged on the economy. Markets were necessary to sell the sacrificial animals and foodstuffs, and all Jews were required to spend ten per cent of their earnings in Jerusalem (the second tithe). How the Temple regulations interacted with political control over other aspects of trade and law is uncertain, although it is clear from historical sources that many "parties" arose who shared quite different understandings of what the role of Hellenic culture should be in the Temple and in Judaism in general.

The final phase of political administration during the Second Temple Period begins with the entry of Pompey into Jerusalem in 63 BCE. Under Roman jurisdiction, control of Judea was split between the Roman appointed ruler and the Sanhedrin, seventy respected members of the Jewish community responsible for overseeing religious law and behavior. Roman rule brought to an end the independent Jewish state and, in 70 CE the Roman destruction of the Temple brought to an end the Second Temple Period and Jerusalem as the religious and political center of Judaism.

Recent excavations in the Jewish Quarter directly opposite and overlooking the sacred precinct have yielded the remains of an affluent district composed of large and finely decorated homes. These homes are primarily attributed to the Hasmonean and Early Roman Periods; their architectural style and content (mosaics, frescoes) vividly illustrate the influence of Hellenization. To date, no Persian or early Hellenistic homes have come to light in this part of the city.

Of the many homes whose great size and fine furnishings suggest that they were the homes of the affluent, is one home known as the "Herodian House." This house was found beneath a well-paved street from late Herodian times that ran from west to east toward the corner of the Temple enclosure. It may have been one of the city's main thoroughfares. Based on coins found in the house it is to be dated to the end of the Hasmonean Period or to the Early Roman Period.

The house was a spacious dwelling occupying some 200 square meters. A series of rooms surrounded an inner courtyard in which four ovens were found. From the courtyard one could descend down a staircase to a pool of water that was perhaps used as a ritual immersion bath (mikveh). Most of the rooms were found empty; evidently they had been cleared out by the residents before it was paved over. The affluence of the family is indicated by the presence of three wall cupboards found in the north wall. The cupboards apparently were used to store and show many of the finer vessels owned by the family. Only broken pots were found by the excavators in the cupboards; however, those that were reconstructed demonstrate the uniqueness of the cupboard space. These objects include red terra sigillata ware (nos. 109,110), a very fine red-slipped pottery that is not commonly found in most homes. This type of pottery was probably initially imported from Italy or France; later it was copied locally, although not with the skill of the foreign artisans.

The "Great House," also found in the Jewish Quarter, was a monumental edifice that testifies to the dramatic impact of Hellenistic culture on the inhabitants of Jerusalem. It was a building of two stories that contained at least thirteen rooms. Frescoes found on the walls of one of the rooms exhibited the same architectural design as frescoes found at the destroyed city of Pompeii, an indication of the diffusion of artistic styles eastward from the Aegean to the Levant. In the room next to the one with the frescoes, was found a floor mosaic with a central square that has a meander pattern surrounding a central circle with pomegrantes in the corners. Pomegrantes, a common Jewish symbol of life (see no. 137), were also found on Jewish coins of the period. A third room, also adjacent to the room with frescoes, was a long hall whose walls were plastered with white stucco in the form of panels. This style of decoration is imitative of "Gaza stone," a sign of wealth and good taste in late Hellenistic times.

The five rooms on the ground floor were all designed with water installations, ranging from a large pool (3.5×4 m., possibly a purification bath) to a small room paved with a white mosaic. Many of the mosaics found in Jerusalem homes from this period were associated with water, presumably as tiling in the rooms where one sat or stood before or after bathing.

A third example of a Jerusalem house is known as the "Burnt House," which came to a sudden fiery end probably during the year that the Temple was destroyed. This dating is confirmed by coins that bear the inscriptions "Year Two," "Year Three" and "Year Four" of the Jewish Revolt that began in 66 CE and resulted in 3 years of independence. This house was much smaller than the two previously discussed, measuring only about 55 square meters. It was composed of an entrance room, four workrooms and a small kitchen. Some of the rooms apparently were used for work related to the production of food, as evidenced by the basalt mortars and pestles (see no. 120), a set of measuring cups (see no. 108), and a set of weights. Inscribed on one of the stone weights was the name Bar Kathros, presumably the owner of the "Burnt House." The "House of Kathros" is known from the Babylonian Talmud as a priestly family in the time of the Second Temple. Here then might be evidence for ascribing this well-made house in close proximity to the Temple Mount to one of the Temple priests. Other finds in the house include an inkwell similar to those found at Qumran (the community of the Dead Sea Scrolls), indicating the advanced education of its inhabitants, and two rectangular stone tables with decorated borders. These tables were used as serving tables upon which such objects as ladles, spoons and pitchers were placed (see nos. 85–87). Beneath the table stood large storage jars, some of which contained wine and water, others containing dry foods (see nos. 83–84).

It is clear that these homes were typical of the affluent; few could afford to own or maintain a two story house or to possess fine objects of glass or terra sigillata. Perhaps even more indicative of the social status of the owners of these homes is their close proximity to the Temple and palace. Most assuredly, this choice location was reserved for high officials, military officers, the priests, or the very wealthy. This was the aristocracy of the time, the people principally affected by Hellenization as evidenced by their ready adoption of frescoes and mosaics in imitation of established Greek traditions.

The closeness of these homes to the Temple may also signal that they were inhabited by observant Jews. This view is supported by the discovery of a ritual bath (mikveh) in almost every excavated home in the Jewish Quarter. One unique find in a home of the Herodian Period was a menorah on a plastered piece of wall, one of the earliest known examples of this distinctly Jewish symbol.

How much Hellenization affected the homes of people far away from Jerusalem is difficult to judge on the scant archaeological evidence. Reactions to the new era were probably mixed among the Jews, as they had been from the days of the Exile, when the culture of Babylon began to amalgamate with the traditional Israelite ways. Some, like the aristocracy, embraced Hellenistic culture; others, like the community of Jews who migrated to the wilderness by the Dead Sea, rejected Hellenization and strove for greater simplicity in their lifestyle devoted to adherence to the Written Law. We may presume that the many colors of the spectrum between these two extremes were well represented. Unfortunately, they have left little evidence for the archaeologist.

Religion (Nos. 116–122)

In many ways, the development of religion in ancient Israel is inextricably tied to the political events of the day. From the days of the Exile, Jerusalem had become a symbol of both national identity and of hopes for the reestablishment of centralized religion. The return from captivity and the subsequent rebuilding of the Temple and repopulation of Jerusalem while under foreign domination resulted in a unique blend of religious and political administration in Judea. This is especially so during the Hasmonean dynasty, when independent Jewish rulers combined the role of king and high priest.

On a functional level, administration of the state's economy and the support of the Temple often overlapped, as when King Herod used Temple funds for construction projects. One result of the close relationship between religion and state was the polarization of different Jewish groups. One camp preferred to have the priesthood and religious affairs separate from the political hierarchy of the state, especially because the state under the Hasmoneans became more and more Hellenized. This camp was opposed by those who profited from the status quo and sought to maintain their aristocratic position.

For the majority of Jews in Judea, and for those living outside the Levant, the center of Judaism was the Temple, not merely in terms of the annual pilgrimage for one of the three feasts (Passover, *Shavuot* or *Sukkot*), or the required tithe set aside for the Temple tax. The Temple represented the heart of Jewish religion and culture and was the connecting link for Jews all over the known world. Thus, when the Temple was destroyed in 70 CE more than the nexus of the religion was destroyed, much of the binding spirit of the people as a whole was also eliminated.

The Temple as it was rebuilt under the guidance of Zerubabel and Nehemiah in the sixth and fifth centuries BCE was probably a modest affair. Following the capture of Jerusalem by the Maccabees, the Temple walls were strengthened so that they were the highest fortifications in the city. However, the major expansion and aggrandizement of the Temple took place under Herod the Great. Herod doubled the size of the Temple Mount and gave it the trapezoidal shape that is still evident today. He also added a retaining wall around the perimeter of the Temple precinct, the western side of which has survived until today as the Western (Wailing) Wall.

The rituals conducted within the Temple are understood primarily through historical sources; archaeology can only reveal pictorial representations of ritual objects. Two examples are the *menorah* found on a marble sacophagus (no. 131) or the *menorah* incised into a plastered wall in one of the homes from the Herodian Period in the Jewish Quarter.

The main ritual of the Temple was sacrifice. Priests officiated two daily offerings that included the sacrifice of a pair of lambs and a libation of wine. Priests also acted as intermediaries for individuals offering a sacrifice, be it a sacrifice of free will, burnt offering, peace offering, thanks offering or a meal offering. Obligatory offerings were conducted by the priests for people who sinned, were guilty or in need of purification.

Ritual purity was required for the wine, flour and oil offerings made by individuals. Thus, these commodities were available for purchase near the Temple. The finest quality of flour was needed for Temple use and it was acquired primarily from the family of Garmo (see no. 120 for the type of mortar and pestle used to prepare grain). The production of incense, which burned in the Temple during the morning and evening offerings, was also the hereditary right of one family. Shovels were used to transport burning coals from the sacrificial altar to the incense altar.

Markets for sacrificial animals existed in close proximity to the Temple so that daily visitors or those visiting on one of the three pilgrimage holidays could purchase animals to bring to the Temple. On the Mount of Olives were four shops that sold things necessary for the sacrifices of purification, perhaps including doves, lambs, sheep, oil, and meal. Of the three pilgrimage holidays Passover was certainly the most crowded in Jerusalem. Jospehus records that the daily offering during the Passover feast was two bulls, one ram, and seven lambs for burnt-offering, and one kid as a sin offering (Antiquities 3.249).

In order to purchase these or other offerings people had to convert their local currency into Temple currency. Money changers were probably located near to the market, offering to accept foreign coins in exchange for the silver Tyrian shekel, the accepted coin of the Temple (no. 116) because of its reliable silver content.

Although the Temple was ostensibly the only

legitimate cultic place for Jews, some local shrines or temples may have existed. A group that was opposed to the Hellenization of the Temple in Jerusalem was the community of Jews who settled at Khirbet Qumran on the shores of the Dead Sea. The famous scrolls which they hid in caves and the austerity of their settlement are well documented. From their writings, it is clear that this was a sect that rejected the priesthood in Jerusalem and the Hellenistic influences on the cult. They set out to form a community based on a covenant of worship that governed their daily lives. The excavations of Qumran have revealed that during the period of the Hasmoneans the Dead Sea community probably resided in caves, reserving the formal structures for places of communal study and prayer. No objects of specifically ritual nature were recovered; however, the extremely careful burial of animal bones may signify that a ritual meal was part of the Qumran religious life. The Qumran community undoubtedly represents one group of Jews who were dissatisfied with the formal practice of the religion as it existed in Jerusalem; they are probably to be identified with the Essenes, a separatist sect mentioned in the writings of Josephus.

Our knowledge of local religious practices is limited to a small number of finds in private dwellings in Jerusalem. Recent excavations in the Jewish Quarter have revealed that almost every house had at least one water installation that may have been used for ritual purification. In fact, some houses had a whole floor devoted to just baths and rooms connected to rituals or activities associated with water. Based on the size and construction of these installations they may have been *mikva'ot*, baths used to wash away impurities caused by impure actions, thoughts or emissions from the body. Similar installations have been discovered at the wilderness site of Masada and the Hasmonean settlement at Gezer.

With the destruction of the Temple in Jerusalem sacrifice as a central part of Jewish ritual came to an end. Synagogues, which probably co-existed with the Temple, took on the burden of being the primary religious organization in Israel and in the Diaspora. The priesthood, once the protectors of Judaism's most sacred rituals, was without a Temple and their role in society as religious leaders was absorbed by the "teachers," later to be known as rabbis. Thus ushered in a new period in Jewish history, one that was not centralized in the Jerusalem Temple but was focused on the individual community.

68   69

68. Coin of Alexander Jannaeus (Yehonatan)

Jerusalem
Hasmonean Period, 103–76 BCE
Bronze: cast and stamped
Diam. 1.3 cm., wt. 1.4 gm.
Provenance unknown
Gift of Samuel Friedenberg   U 7531

Obverse inscription in ancient Hebrew:
  Yhwntn Hmlkh
  Yehonatan the King.
Reverse inscription in Greek:
  ΒΑΣ[ΙΛΕΩΣ] ΑΛΕΞΑΝΔ[ΡΩΥ]
  [Of] Alexand[er] the Ki[ng].

Alexander Jannaeus (in Hebrew, Yehonatan)
served as king and high priest in Judea from 103
to 76 BCE. He was a member of the Hasmonean
dynasty which fought for and gained both
religious freedom and nationhood from the
Seleucid overlords. Alexander expanded the
borders of the Jewish kingdom through his
military campaigns until they nearly reached the
extent of Solomon's domain. He was also the first
Hasmonean king to mint his own coins, the
earlier ones based on Greek Judean prototypes
and the later ones with strictly Jewish symbols
such as the pomegranate.

Description: obverse: star with ancient Hebrew
inscription between rays; reverse: anchor with Greek
inscription.
Parallels: Meshorer 1967: no. 8; Hendin 1976: no. 10.

69. Coin of John Hyrcanus II (Yehoḥanan)

Jerusalem
Early Roman Period, 63–40 BCE
Bronze: cast and stamped
Length 1.4 cm., wt. 1.2 gm.
Purchased in Israel
Gift of the Betty and Max Ratner Collection   1981–192

Obverse inscription in ancient Hebrew:
  Yhḥnn hkhn hgdl vr'š hvr hyhdym
  Yehoḥanan the High Priest and Head of the Council of the Jews.

The stories recorded of the Hasmonean kings are
filled with grisly incidents of massacre and family
in-fighting, and the reign of John Hyrcanus II was
no exception. Constant struggles between
Hyrcanus and his younger brother Aristobulus
led to Roman intervention on behalf of Hyrcanus.
The Romans had by then eclipsed the Greeks in
their political influence over the Levant.
Hyrcanus was reinstalled as high priest of Judah
but stripped of the title of king, and many of the
coastal and Transjordanian cities were annexed
by the Romans. Thus ended the brief resurgence
of the independent Jewish state during the
Second Temple Period.

Description: obverse: ancient Hebrew inscription in
wreath; reverse: double cornucopia with pomegranate
between horns.
Bibliography: Kozloff 1978: no. RC 151.
Parallels: Meshorer 1967: no. 23; Hendin 1976: no. 27.

70. Jar Handle with Seal Impression

Rhodes
Hellenistic Period, ca. 220–180 BCE
Clay: body wheel-turned, handle pulled, stamped,
  slipped, fired
Handle width 4.3 cm., handle length 7.1 cm.
Purchased in Israel, 1981
Gift of the Betty and Max Ratner Collection   1982-20

Greek inscription:
Ε[ΠΙ Α]ΙΝΗΣΙ[ΔΑ]ΜΟΥ ΠΑΝΑΜΟΥ
[In the] y[ear] of [A]inesi[da]mos, [in
the month of] Panamos.

This handle bears a common type of stamped
inscription, with the name of a specific priest of
Rhodes and the month that the wine inside the
jar was bottled. Separate epigraphic sources have
provided lists of these high priests and enable us
to determine when they served as head of the
priesthood. The jar handle shown here bears the
name of Ainesidamos; another example with the
same name was excavated in the Tyropoeon
Valley of Jerusalem, and can be dated to the end
of the 3rd century to the mid-2nd century BCE.

Rhodian wine would have been considered by
Jews as "libation wine," (i.e., consecrated for
ritual use by non-Jews) and consequently not
kosher (see also no. 83). This may explain why so
few Rhodian jar handles were found in the
Upper City (Jewish Quarter excavations) of
Jerusalem, which was adjacent to the Temple and
may have been occupied by at least one priestly
family (Avigad 1980: 79, 130).

Description: neck fragment straight-sided; rim
slightly thickened on interior, exterior thickened and
molded; handle has oval cross-section, coming to elbow
bend, broken below bend. Rectangular stamp
impression on top of handle, with three lines of Greek
inscription, the first and second incomplete. Orange-
buff ware; buff slip.
Parallels: Nachtergael 1978, vol. I: fig. 12; Crowfoot
and Fitzgerald 1927: 86, fig. 1:4 (Jerusalem).

71. Jar Handle with Seal Impression

Rhodes
Late Hellenistic Period, ca. 110–80 BCE
Clay: body wheel-turned, handle pulled, slipped, fired
Handle length 8.8 cm., handle width 4.4 cm.
Purchased in Israel, 1981
Gift of the Betty and Max Ratner Collection   1982-21

Greek inscription:
ΜΕΝΑΝΔΡΟΥ Δ[Ι]ΟΣΘΥΟΥ
[Of] Menandros [in the month of] D[i]osthuos.

In Israel, these stamped handles from large
storage jars are frequently found at excavated
sites. For example, they were numerous in the
City of David (Jerusalem), although scarce in the
excavations of the Upper City (Avigad 1980: 79).
The inscription bearing the name of the vintner
(in this case, Menandros) and the decorative
motif, the rose, indicate that the jars and their
wine contents came from Rhodes, which had an
active wine trade in the eastern Mediterranean
from the 3rd to the 1st centuries BCE.

Description: neck fragment: rolled rim, straight
interior, exterior thickened and molded; handle has
oval cross section, and elbow bend, broken below
bend. Circular stamp impression on top of handle with
Greek inscription written backward around
circumference, and three-petaled rose in center.
Orange-buff clay, slip same.
Parallels: Grace 1965: 15.

70

71

72. Spindle Bottle

Eastern Mediterranean, probably Israel
Hasmonean Period, ca. 150–20 BCE
Clay: wheel-turned, slipped, burnished, fired
Ht. 11.5 cm., diam. 4.1 cm.
Purchased in Israel
Gift of the Betty and Max Ratner Collection   1981–135

These long, thin vessels, common in Israel during
the Hasmonean Period, originate directly from
Greek forms of the 4th–3rd centuries BCE.
Sometimes called fusiform bottles or unguentaria,
they may have been used to hold oils or scent.

Description: globular mid-section, slightly off-center;
slight carination at shoulder; cylindrical neck; cup-like
rim (convex-sided) with interior groove, molded on
exterior; mid-section narrows into tall cylindrical foot
with flared bottom; flat base with square, exterior
molding.
Bibliography: Kozloff 1978: no. RC 93.
Parallels: Lapp 1964: pl. 77:1–11 (Tell el-Fûl); *Ashdod
I:* fig. 4:5; Thompson 1934: fig. 15:B6, fig. 78:D78;
Mazar 1971: 31:19–24; 33:31,32 (Jerusalem); Avigad
1980: pl. 59 (Jerusalem); *Bethany:* fig. 45:1; *Gezer I:* pl.
33.26; *Tell en-Nasbeh II:* pl. 75:1733.

72

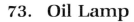

73

74

73. Oil Lamp

Israel
Late Persian–Early Roman Period, 4th–1st cent. BCE
Clay: wheel-turned, folded, fired
Ht. 3.1 cm., length 8.7 cm., width 5.3 cm.
Purchased in Israel
Gift of the Betty and Max Ratner Collection   1981–134

Small, folded lamps of this type developed from
the open saucers with pinched spouts of the Iron
Age and Early Persian Period (see nos. 13, 36,
and 37). The innovation occurred in Greece in
the 5th century BCE, when the folds of the earlier
saucer types were closed together, preventing the
oil inside from spilling (Sussman 1972: 20). The
folded lamp has a long period of use in Israel,
gradually replacing the Iron Age pinched
spout types and still used alongside the wheel-
made closed lamps of the 1st century BCE
(no. 74).

Description: bowl-shaped body with two edges
folded toward center and touching; small wick hole on
spout and larger fill hole; very low disc base. Red
ware; buff slip.
Bibliography: Kozloff 1978: no. RC 92.
Parallels: Mazar and Dothan 1966: fig. 25:9 (Tell
Goren); *Ramat Rahel II:* fig. 11:5; Rahmani 1980: pl.
VII:1 (Mt. Scopus tomb); Mazar 1971: 31:27 (Jerusalem);
Avigad 1980: fig. 70 (Jerusalem).

74. Oil Lamp

Probably Israel
Probably Hasmonean Period, 2nd–1st cent. BCE
Clay: wheel-turned, slipped, fired
Ht. 3.5 cm., diam. 7.1 cm.
Provenance unknown
T11

The transition from the folded lamp (no. 73) to
the wheel-made, closed-bowl lamp occurred in
Greece in the 4th century BCE and spread to the
coastal sites of Israel through sea trade (Sussman
1972: 21). The closed form with flat base is
obviously more stable than the open saucers,
from which oil could easily be spilled.
While the general shape of this lamp places it
with the group of Hellenistic lamps called
delphiniform, the bowl-like shape of the wick
hole suggests it may be transitional to the short-
nozzled lamps of the Roman period.

Description: round, closed bowl with convex sides,
large fill hole in center of top surrounded by slight
ridge; remains of loop handle at back; conical applied
nozzle ends in a bowl-like wick hole which rises higher
than the body; low disc base. Coarse red ware; buff
slip.
Parallels: *Corinth IV, pt. II:* fig. 33 *de Vaux 1954:* fig.
2:15 (*Khirbet Qumran*); Lapp 1964: fig. 46:7 (Tell el-Fûl).

75. Aryballos

Eastern Mediterranean
Persian–Early Hellenistic Periods, 6th–4th cent. BCE
Glass: core-formed, marvered, thread handle
Ht. 6 cm., diam. 4.3 cm.
Purchased in Israel
Gift of Elaine and Harvey Rothenberg   1979–91

Aryballoi of pottery were used by athletes as containers for rubbing oil, although the more delicate glass ones may have contained perfumes (Auth 1976: 33). Later examples of blown glass aryballoi (from the 1st–2nd centuries CE) have chains or handles so they could be worn to the bath, and one such example was found in Israel (Auth 1976: 118). These contained oil to be rubbed on the body and then scraped down with a metal strygil, which was the method of bathing before the use of soap. Several gold and glass stands for aryballoi have survived from antiquity, indicating how these vessels were supported on their round bottoms.

Description: ovoid body, coming to blunt point at bottom; cylindrical neck; rim folded out and over; handles curl at bottom and are pierced; vertical ribbing on upper body. White matrix with cream chevrons on shoulder accented with dark blue, two horizontal cream bands below, thin traces of dark blue in upper body and neck.

Parallels: Barag 1966 (Ein Gedi); Auth 1976: no. 16; Matheson 1980: nos. 10,11.

75

Hellenistic Core-Formed Glass

The spread of Greek art forms to Israel is evident in the appearance, even before the Hellenistic Period, of core-made glass vessels of four basic shapes: the aryballos, amphoriskos, alabastron, and oenichoe. The names and the shapes of these vessel types come from Greek pottery. They were produced by the earliest method of glass manufacture, in which a core of sand, mud, or clay was dipped into molten glass, and different colored glass threads were rolled into the surface as decoration (marvering).

Core-made glass began to appear in tombs in Israel during the Iron Age in the late 7th century BCE (Barag 1966). The paucity of identifiable fragments of this type of glass in excavation strata of the 6th–3rd centuries BCE suggests that core-made glass was still a luxury import in Israel at that time (Barag 1971a: 202, fig 105:14 (Ashdod); G. Weinberg 1970: 18 (Tell Anafa); *Samaria-Sebaste III*: 402). Scholars differ over the place of manufacture of these glass vessels, and centers in Egypt, Greece, and Phoenicia have been proposed, although to date the only evidence we have of a glass factory from this early phase is possibly at Rhodes.

76

77

76. Amphoriskos

Eastern Mediterranean
Late Hellenistic Period, 2nd–1st cent. BCE
Glass: core-formed, marvered, thread handles
Ht. 8.3 cm., width at handles 4.4 cm.
Purchased in Israel
Gift of Judith Riklis   1981–293

These long, pointed, two-handled jars (nos. 76,77)
are generally thought to have held perfume, as
represented in a Roman fresco of a woman
pouring a liquid from a round jug into an
amphoriskos (Schoder n.d.: pl. 88A).

Description: ovoid body with pronounced shoulder;
tall narrow neck; rim folded out and over; drop base;
two handles. White thread wound into black matrix;
the thread begins at the neck and creates diagonal and
horizontal bands, some straight and others zig-zag,
finally curling around base.
Parallels: Hayes 1975: no. 33; Auth 1976: nos. 22,23.

77. Amphoriskos

Eastern Mediterranean
Late Hellenistic Period, 1st cent. BCE
Glass: core-formed, marvered, thread handles
Ht. 11.2 cm., diam. 7.5 cm.
Purchased in Israel
Gift of Elaine and Harvey Rothenberg   1979–92

Description: ovoid body, widest at shoulder; tall neck
constricted below rim; rim folded out and over; two
thread handles of medium translucent blue; button
base, medium blue, is an added, flattened glass knob.
Dark blue body with yellow threads, white added at
shoulder in a feather pattern; horizontal bands on neck
and lower body.
Parallels: Auth 1976: no. 281.

79

78. Ribbed Bowl

Eastern Mediterranean
Late Hellenistic Period, 2nd–1st cent. BCE
Glass: mold-pressed and wheel-incised
Ht. 5.7 cm., diam. 11.5 cm.
Provenance unknown
Loaned by Daniel M. Friedenberg   L1982-3.4

In the Late Hellenistic Period, another form of glass-making, the pressing of bowls in molds, was developed and a translucent glass came into use. Two types of mold-pressed bowls are found: the first is mainly conical in form and has interior wheel-incised bands, while the second has vertical sides and vertical exterior ribs in addition to the interior bands.

These bowls are the most commonly found glass vessels in excavation strata in Israel (e.g., at Ashdod, Samaria-Sebaste, Nessena, Tell Anafa, and Jerusalem). In Jerusalem, fragments of both the plain and the ribbed bowls were the major components of the glass debris that is believed to have been dumped from a nearby factory into an abandoned purification bath, around 50 BCE.

The large number of these glass bowls at sites like Tell Anafa, when glass was usually scarce, has led to the suggestion that they belonged to a rich household that entertained frequently (G. Weinberg 1970: 27). The bowls evidently were meant for table ware, the larger ones for food and the smaller perhaps for drink.

Description: vertical-sided bowl diverging slightly toward rim; low vertical ribs closely spaced on exterior of body, slightly diagonal in direction with oval cross-section; wheel-incised band on interior rim, and two bands below interior midpoint; rim straight and fire-polished; base flat.
Parallels: G. Weinberg 1970: profile nos. 31,32 (Tell Anafa); *Ashdod II–III:* pl. 98:7,9; Avigad 1980: fig. 220 (Jerusalem).

79. Head of a Woman

Eastern Mediterranean
Probably Middle Roman Period, 1st–2nd cent. CE
Clay: mold-formed, slipped, fired
Ht. 11.2 cm., width 9.2 cm., depth 8.5 cm.
Purchased in Israel
Gift of the Betty and Max Ratner Collection   1981-137

This head, although probably of Roman Period date, is imitative of earlier Hellenistic types. The figure is possibly wearing an ivy wreath, which is connected with the Greek god Dionysus, whose cult becomes extremely popular in Late Hellenistic and Roman times in the eastern Mediterranean, even reaching as far as Iran. The style of hair and the treatment of the eyes are perhaps more characteristic of Roman work.

These terra cotta heads were meant as votive offerings at pagan temples, and numerous examples of Greek, Cypriot, and Roman figures and heads have been excavated in Israel. Many seem to be concentrated in *favissae,* pits outside sanctuaries where ritual objects no longer needed are buried. One such deposit was discovered at Tell Sippor on the coast; mineralogical, stylistic, and chronological analyses have suggested that the objects came from a possible Phoenician sanctuary on the site in the 6th to 4th centuries BCE (Negbi 1966: 9). A whole room filled with

Roman-style terra cotta heads (probably a shop) was found at Gerasa in Jordan (Illife 1944). It is not clear who was purchasing these votive heads, but they were probably intended for non-Jewish sanctuaries.

Description: hollow head and neck of a woman wearing a leafy crown, probably an ivy wreath; hair depicted in concave waves around the face, and appears to be covered by a net in back; round earrings; neck is irregular on bottom with several grooved marks; vent-hole on top of head. Object caught inside the head makes a rattling noise, but could have fallen inside during the modern repair; light brown ware; traces of white slip.
Bibliography: Kozloff 1978: no. RC 95, fig. 44.
Parallels: Wegner 1939: pl. 12 (Dresden), pl. 34 (Rome, Capitoline); Mattingly 1940; vol. IV: BMC 1058,1063,1089. For use in Israel: Avigad 1980: fig. 250 (Jerusalem); Iliffe 1944.

80. Ear or Nose Ring

Eastern Mediterranean
Probably Hellenistic Period, 4th–1st cent. BCE
Gold: cast, granulated, cut sheet metal, twisted wire
Diam. 1.4 cm., head diam. 0.4 cm.
Purchased in Israel
Gift of the Betty and Max Ratner Collection   1981–131

Israelite jewelry usually incorporated simple, mostly undecorated forms. However, lions' heads are popular decorative elements in eastern Mediterranean jewelry of the Persian, Hellenistic, and Roman Periods. The ibex or antelope horns on the lion finial of this hoop are possibly intended to represent a lion-griffin. This mythical creature, part lion, horned animal, and bird, is particularly common in Persian art of the Achaemenid Period (6th–4th centuries BCE).

Description: lion head with hollow, drooping eyes, open mouth, mane depicted in two rows of horizontal curls; ears tiny and pointed; horns curve upward and then down to touch the collar, curled on end, horizontally incised; small rectangular knob on top of head; collar of several rings, one granulated. Two wires attached to an inner tube emanate from hole below lion's mouth and curve under chin to hold head to rest of ring (possibly a modern repair). Hoop made of five wires twisted into a narrowing spiral, held on the wide end by three rings: one scalloped, one with four ribs, and one plain. An inner tube connects the head to the hoop and is probably a modern addition; end of hoop missing.
Bibliography: Kozloff 1978: no. RC 89, fig. 45.
Parallels: *Swedish Cyprus Expedition IV, pt. 2:* fig. 34:27; Alexander 1928: fig. 38,39; Griefenhagen 1970: pl. 22:1; Hoffmann and Davidson 1966: fig. 25; Higgins 1961: pl. 51:13 (Capua).

81. Pair of Earrings

Eastern Mediterranean
Hellenistic to Early Roman Periods, 4th cent. BCE–1st cent. CE
Gold: hammered, granulated, drawn wire
Length 2.85 cm., width 1.3 cm.
Purchased in Israel
Gift of the Betty and Max Ratner Collection   1981–211,212

Description: each earring consists of two vertical circles of sheet gold (forming a figure 8) with convex surfaces; row of five small granules attached between the two circles; ear wire attached in center of upper circle ending in a hoop; closes into loop at bottom of lower circle.
Bibliography: Kozloff 1978: no. RC 169 A,B, color pl. 6.
Parallels: Harding 1951: pl. IX:38 (Amman tomb); Overbeck 1856: fig. 286 (Pompeii).

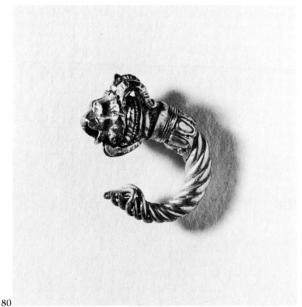

80

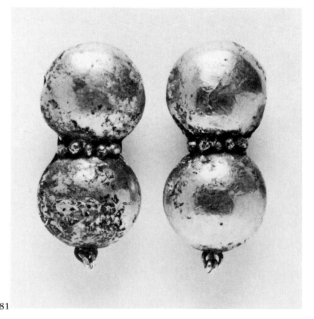

81

82

82. Helmet

Greece
Greek Archaic–Classical Periods, 9th–5th cent. BCE
Bronze: hammered and drilled
Ht. 23 cm., diam. 17.5 cm.
Provenance unknown
Loaned by the Joseph Ternbach Collection L1982–3.8

This helmet, while not actually from the Hasmonean/Hellenistic Period, can be considered as symbolic of the Greek conquests of the Near East in the late 4th century BCE. The discovery of such a helmet in the waters off the coast of Israel (Radan 1961) is indicative of the contact between the Levant and Greece before the actual conquests. This helmet may have belonged to a soldier accompanying a trading vessel from the Aegean. Corinthian style helmets were, however, sometimes made as special orders during the Roman period for parade wear.

The perforations around the lower edge were meant for the attachment of a leather lining for added protection and comfort, while the perforations at the top and back were probably intended for mounting a crest.

Description: globular-shape, narrowing slightly at the base; teardrop-shaped nose piece; perforations on all helmet edges; two perforations on top of crown, one small perforated rectangular horizontal knob on exterior of back of lower part of helmet.
Parallels: Radan 1961: pl. 36:A; McClees 1941: fig. 107; *Swedish Cyprus Expedition IV, pt. 2:* pl. XVI; Levi 1980: 63 (Dodona), 68,92 (Sparta), 122,135.

83. Large Transport Amphora

Probably Italy
Early–Middle Roman Period, 1st cent. BCE–2nd cent. CE
Clay: hand-coiled, rolled handles, slipped, fired
Ht. 104.5 cm., diam. 28.6 cm.
Purchased in Israel, 1981
Gift of the Betty and Max Ratner Collection   1982–27

In the late 1st century BCE, large storage jars with
pointed bottoms and often with Latin inscriptions
stamped on their handles began to appear in
Israel. These are evidence of an extensive
shipping trade under the Roman Empire, which
reached ports from Spain to Syria and Israel and
beyond (Casson 1981: 39). The chief product
being exported from Italy was wine and the
amphorae were primarily made at each vineyard
and filled, ready for shipping.

A number of these amphorae came from Early
Roman Period houses excavated in the Jewish
Quarter in Jerusalem in addition to other sites
like Beth Shan. If the jars did in fact contain
imported wine, then the liquid could not have
been used for ritual libation by Jews, for wine
consecrated by non-Jews for idol worship (called
"libation wine") was forbidden for this purpose.
However, until Talmudic times it could be used
for everyday consumption purposes, particularly
if it were boiled or mixed and/or diluted with
prescribed amounts of other substances (*Avodah
Zarah* 29b).

Description: long conical body tapering toward
bottom, angled more sharply just above truncated
conical base; long, fairly straight neck widening toward
steeply sloped shoulder; rim slightly flared with flat top
sloping downward to exterior, and exterior and
interior thickening; handles have round cross-section.
Light brown-gray ware; buff-pink slip.
Parallels: Avigad 1980: figs. 69,129 (Jerusalem); Tsori
1977 (Beth Shan); Callendar 1965: IId (Kent, England);
Netzer and Meyers 1977: fig. 9:8 (Jericho).

83

84. Storage Jar (NOT ILLUSTRATED)

Southern Israel
Early–Middle Roman Period, 1st–2nd cent. CE
Clay: wheel-turned, pulled handles, ribbed, fired
Ht. 49 cm., diam. 33.4 cm.
Purchased in Israel
Gift of the Betty and Max Ratner Collection   1981–218

This ribbed jar with broad bottom is the local
storage jar of Roman Period Israel. It was used
for storing wine, oil, grains, fruits, and even
perfume, as is known from an inscription on a
1st century BCE jar (Zevulun and Olenik 1979: no.
247). A representation of a serving table, carved
on a table top found in the Jerusalem vicinity,
depicts large jars under the table, probably
containing wine or other ingredients for a
banquet (Avigad 1980: fig. 194).

Description: pear-shaped body, wider at bottom,
with slightly undulating sides; entire body has
horizontal, spiraling grooves of hemispherical profile
which are slightly more widely spaced at midpoint;
round bottom; rim slightly convex-sided; two opposing
vertical handles at the shoulder with flat cross-section
and central ridge.
Bibliography: Kozloff 1978: no. RC 176.
Parallels: Bar Adon 1977: fig. 10:1 (En el-Ghuweir);
Lapp and Lapp 1974: pl. 24 (Wadi ed-Daliyeh); Avigad
1980: fig. 212 (Jerusalem).

85

85. Jug with Figural Decoration

Eastern Mediterranean
Early—Middle Roman Period, 1st cent. BCE–2nd cent. CE
Bronze: cast and incised
Ht. 16.6 cm., diam. 11 cm.
Purchased in Israel
Gift of the Betty and Max Ratner Collection   1981–86

A cache of bronze vessels, including several of these jugs with human figural decoration, was found in the Cave of the Letters in the Judean desert. It had been hidden during the Bar Kokhba revolt against Rome in 132–135 CE, when the caves were used as refuges by Jewish citizens and warriors. All of the facial features on the jugs had been defaced with incisions or filed smooth, just as on the jug shown here. The excavator suggests that the vessels represent booty taken from Roman soldiers, and that the images were defaced in accordance with the biblical injunction against graven images (*Bar*

Kokhba: 102). The Mishnah informs us that an idol can be desecrated ". . . if a gentile cut off the tip of its ear, or the end of its nose, or the tip of its finger, or battered it even though nought was broken off . . ." (*Avodah Zarah* 4:5).

Several bronze vessels, one possibly with figural decoration, were also discovered in a Roman Period house in the Jewish Quarter of Jerusalem.

Description: piriform body, widest at shoulder; wide flaring neck pinched at rim to form oval mouth; at top end of handle is a human protome (head, chest, and arms); the figure wears a pointed cap, the face has no features, and the arms embrace the rim of the vessel; at base of handle is a face with the features incised and abraded; concave disc base.
Bibliography: Kozloff 1978: no.RC 42A, fig. 47.
Parallels: *Bar Kokhba:* 100–103,110–111; Yadin 1961: 39, pl. 20C (Cave of the Letters); Avigad 1980: figs. 195,234 (Jerusalem); Lapp and Lapp 1974: pls. 35,99 (Wadi ed-Daliyeh).

86. Ladle (NOT ILLUSTRATED)

Probably Israel
Early Roman Period, ca. 1st cent. CE
Bronze: cast and incised
Ht. 13.3 cm., diam. of bowl 5.2 cm.
Purchased in Israel
Gift of the Betty and Max Ratner Collection   1981–123

An unstratified stone table top found in the Jerusalem vicinity is decorated with a depiction of a table bearing the numerous serving vessels necessary for a meal. Among the vessels is a ladle similar to this Jewish Museum example and also to one excavated in the Jewish Quarter of Jerusalem.

Description: convex-sided bowl with flat bottom; flat upright handle is cut out on top into a flat lozenge shape with knob at end; base has two incised concentric circles; incised bands on rim of bowl, midpoint, and top of handle; part of bowl missing.
Bibliography: Kozloff 1978: no. RC 81.
Parallels: Avigad 1980: fig. 173 (Jerusalem); Richter 1915: nos. 653,654; de Franciscis 1963: fig. 1 (Herculaneum).

87. Spoon (NOT ILLUSTRATED)

Eastern Mediterranean
Early Roman Period, 1st cent. CE
Bronze: cast
Length 13.4 cm., width 3.4 cm.
Purchased in Israel
Gift of the Betty and Max Ratner Collection   1981–95

These spoons, with their angled bend at the base of the handle, are very common in Italian sites, while spoons in general are rare in Israel.

Description: oval bowl; round-sectioned handle with conical knob on end; at join with bowl, handle makes a right angle and becomes square in cross-section.
Bibliography: Kozloff 1978: no. RC 95.
Parallels: Avigad 1980: fig. 235 (Jerusalem); Mau 1899: fig. 196:n,v (Pompeii); McClees 1941: fig. 40; Oliver 1977: no. 69 (reported to be from Tivoli).

88. Ribbed Bowl

Eastern Mediterranean
Early Roman Period, 1st cent. CE
Glass: mold-pressed and wheel-incised
Ht. 5.1 cm., diam. 15.7 cm.
Provenance unknown
Loaned by Daniel M. Friedenberg   L1982–3.5

This ribbed bowl of the Roman Period continues the mold-pressed tradition of the Late Hellenistic ones (cf. no. 78). It can be differentiated from the earlier version by the low sides and more pronounced, widely spaced ribs. A bowl very similar to the piece shown here was discovered in the 1st century CE "Great House" excavated in the Jewish Quarter in Jerusalem. From the same house came a nearly identical bronze bowl, which is possibly the prototype for this kind of ribbed glass bowl (Avigad 1980: fig. 115).

Description: shallow, convex-sided body with vertical external ribs of rounded cross-section, ribs wider on top, narrower below; interior wheel-incised band at rim, and two below midpoint; base flat externally, raised internally; rim fire-polished. Light green color.
Parallels: Avigad 1980: fig. 114 (Jerusalem).

88

Roman Blown Glass

The 1st century BCE witnessed the transition from core- and mold-made glass to that produced by blowing into a glass bulb through a blowpipe. Scholars are uncertain where this technique was invented, for the use of free-blown glass vessels quickly became widespread throughout the eastern Mediterranean world during the late 1st century BCE. The earliest datable examples both come from Israel. A free-blown bottle was discovered in a pre-Herodian cemetery at Ein Gedi and can be dated to ca. 40–37 BCE (Avigad 1962: 183). A second piece comes from a sealed, abandoned ritual bath in the Jewish Quarter excavation in Jerusalem. It contained a large quantity of broken mold-made glass bowls of Late Hellenistic type (cf. no. 78), waste products of glass blowing and fragments of several blown bottles (Avigad 1972: 200). The deposit was dated by its content of Hellenistic pottery and by coins of Alexander Jannaeus, which were used into the Herodian period. It is cited as evidence of the transition from core- and mold-made glass to free-blown, ca. 50 BCE.

These early blown vessels were mainly piriform or spherical bottles. They are rarely found in excavated strata but come more commonly from tombs. It is not certain whether their paucity in occupation levels indicates that their function was primarily to hold funerary offerings of oil or perfume, or whether their fragility prevented them from surviving intact in domestic contexts. The rapidity with which blown glass could be produced, as opposed to the core-formed method, contributed to its adoption by the middle class and the frequency with which it is found in tombs.

89. Large Globular Bottle

Eastern Mediterranean
Middle Roman Period, 2nd–3rd cent. CE
Glass: free-blown
Ht. 25 cm., diam. 19.6 cm.
Purchased in Israel
Gift of the Betty and Max Ratner Collection   1981–79

This long-necked globular bottle is probably the form referred to in the Talmud as the *tzlohit* or flask (Zevulun and Olenik 1979: 18). It functioned much like the modern bottle; the large flasks "held in two hands" were designed to hold wine, which would have been poured into cups during the meal.

Description: globular body; neck constricted where joins shoulder, then curves gently in an S; rim flared, folded out and over, fire-polished; base concave. Light green color, interior iridescence.
Bibliography: Kozloff 1978: no. RC 35, color pl. 8.
Parallels: Hak 1965: fig. 10 (Homs cemetery); Matheson 1980: no. 204; Zevulun and Olenik 1979: no. 65.

90. Cylindrical Jug

Eastern Mediterranean
Middle Roman Period, late 1st–2nd cent. CE
Glass: free-blown, wheel-incised, thread handle
Ht. 19.5 cm., diam. 8 cm.
Purchased in Israel
Gift of the Betty and Max Ratner Collection   1981–70

Although it is difficult to find glass vessels in excavated sites in Israel, a similar cylindrical glass jug was discovered in the Cave of the Letters in the Judean desert. This and other caves were inhabited by Jewish refugees and warriors during the Second Jewish Revolt against Rome in 132–135 CE.

Description: cylindrical body, narrower on bottom; neck constricted where joins shoulder; rim folded down, up, out, and over, flattened; four-rib angled handle; base slightly concave; five wheel-incised bands on body. Bluish green, interior weathering.
Bibliography: Kozloff 1978: no. RC 22.
Parallels: de Franciscis 1963: fig. 3 (Herculaneum); *Bar Kokhba:* 119; Auth 1976: no. 131; Matheson 1980: no. 96.

91. Square Shipping Bottle

Probably Italy
Early–Middle Roman Period, 1st–2nd cent. CE
Glass: mold-blown and thread handle
Ht. 16.8 cm., length 6.8 cm., width 6.6 cm.
Purchased in Israel
Gift of Judith Riklis   1981–289

The square- and hexagonal-shaped jugs with thick walls were ideal for packing and shipping, and they were one of the more common glass forms of the early Roman Empire. Evidence for their function and dating comes from the discovery, in the ruins of a shop at Herculaneum (destroyed 79 CE), of a set of square jugs packed in straw in partitioned boxes ready for shipping. Archaeologists have not yet found any shipping bottles with their contents intact, and so we cannot be certain what was being sent around the eastern Mediterranean.

Description: square body with round shoulder; cylindrical neck; rim folded out, over and down, and flattened; eight-ribbed handle with sharp bend; mark on bottom: center dot with three concentric circles and chevron in each corner, flat uneven surface. Light blue glass.
Parallels: de Franciscis 1963: fig. 4 (Herculaneum); Auth 1976: no. 128; Matheson 1980: no. 95; Charlesworth 1966: fig. 3 (similar mark).

89

90

91

92. Hexagonal Shipping Bottle

Eastern Mediterranean
Early—Middle Roman Period, 1st—2nd cent. CE
Glass: free-blown and flattened
Ht. 15.6 cm., width 8.6 cm.
Purchased in Israel
Gift of the Betty and Max Ratner Collection   1981–169

Description: unequal-sided hexagonal body; round
shoulder; cylindrical neck wider at bottom; rim folded
out, over, and flattened; double-ribbed handle; uneven
base with concavity and traces of hexagonal outline.
Bluish green with iridescent surface areas.
Bibliography: Kozloff 1978: no. RC 128.
Parallels: de Franciscis 1963: fig. 4 (Herculaneum);
Auth 1976: no. 129.

93. Bottle

Eastern Mediterranean
Early—Middle Roman Period, late 1st–3rd cent. CE
Glass: free-blown and wheel-incised
Ht. 14.5 cm., diam. 10.2 cm.
Purchased in Israel
Gift of the Betty and Max Ratner Collection   1981–72

93

The bright green color and wheel-incised bands
of this bottle suggest a 1st century CE date;
however, its form is generally found in later
contexts.

Description: globular body; funnel-shaped neck; rim
sharp and unworked; base concave. Green color,
horizontal wheel-incised bands on rim, neck, and body.
Bibliography: Kozloff 1978: no. RC 26.
Parallels: Kahane 1961: fig. 4:3 (Huqoq tombs); Barag
1962: 212, fig. 12 (Cave of Horror); *Samaria-Sebaste III:*
pl. 95:8.

94. Globular Bottle

Eastern Mediterranean
Early Roman Period, 1st cent. CE
Glass: free-blown
Ht. 10.9 cm., diam. 6.6 cm.
Purchased in Israel
Gift of Judith Riklis   1981–273

Description: flattened globular body; tall cylindrical
neck constricted at base, flaring at mouth; rim folded
out and over; base concave. Purple color.
Parallels: Matheson 1980: no. 75.

94

95

95. Globular Bottle

Eastern Mediterranean
Early Roman Period, 1st cent. CE
Glass: free-blown and wheel-incised
Ht. 12.1 cm., diam. 6.8 cm.
Purchased in Israel
Gift of Judith Riklis   1981–269

Description: globular body; tall cylindrical neck widens slightly at base; rim folded out and over; base slightly concave. Light blue color, horizontal incised bands on body, traces of iridescence.
Parallels: Matheson 1980: no. 74; Grose 1977: 26 (Lipari).

96. Piriform Bottle

Eastern Mediterranean
Early Roman Period, 1st cent. CE
Glass: free-blown
Ht. 10.5 cm., diam. 6.8 cm.
Purchased in Israel
Gift of the Betty and Max Ratner Collection   1981–83

The use of deep colors in glassware, like this bottle and nos. 93 to 95, seems to be confined to the 1st century CE as cited by Strabo and Pliny the Elder (Matheson 1980: xiii). Subsequently the clearer, pale blue or green-tinged glass was favored (Hayes 1975: 34, see nos. 89–92). Not many stratified examples of colored transparent glass come from Israel, but colored vessels of this shape are well-attested to in Italian sites and burials of the 1st century CE.

Description: piriform body, cylindrical neck with

slight incision at its base; rim everted and flat, fire-polished; base flat. Deep blue color, some weathering.
Bibliography: Kozloff 1978: no. RC 39, fig. 55.
Parallels: *Samaria-Sebaste III:* fig. 93:7; Grose 1977: figs. 7,8 (Italy); Harden 1969: pl. 1:D (Italy); Matheson 1980: no. 81.

97. Piriform Bottle

Eastern Mediterranean
Early Roman Period, early 1st cent. BCE
Glass: free-blown and banded
Ht. 10.1 cm., diam. 4.6 cm.
Purchased in New York
Gift of Elaine and Harvey Rothenberg   1979–94

This vessel was decorated by placing colored glass threads on the surface and allowing them to expand while the vessel was blown (banding). This is thought to be a cheap imitation of mosaic glass, in which the colors are mixed within the glass matrix, and are not just laid on the surface. The same piriform shape is also found in clay bottles of the Early Roman Period (cf. nos. 111, 112).

Description: piriform body; flat base with punty mark; cylindrical neck with slight constriction where joins body; everted rim folded out and over. Light green glass, surface decoration of white and gold in large festoon pattern.
Parallels: Avigad 1980: 127,186, figs. 124,221 (Jerusalem); Barag 1962: 183 (Ein Gedi); Fortuna 1965: figs. 2,4 (Akko tombs); Rahmani 1961: 116, pl. 17:6 (Jerusalem tombs).

96

97

98

98. Jar

Eastern Mediterranean
Early Roman Period, 1st cent. CE
Glass: mold-blown and thread handles
Ht. 9 cm., diam. 4.4 cm.
Purchased in Israel
Gift of Elaine and Harvey Rothenberg   1979–93

Another technique of glass making, developed
during the 1st century CE, was that of
mold-blowing. The vessel was blown into
a two-part mold, which produced the relief
design. The seam between the two halves of the
mold can be clearly seen in the Jewish Museum
vessel. The technique is believed to have
originated near Sidon, where a well-known glass
maker named Ennion, who signed his products,
seems to have had his 1st century CE workshop.
Three or four of his signed mold-blown vases
were recovered in the Early Roman "Great House"
excavated in the Jewish Quarter of Jerusalem.

Description: oval body; misshapen cylindrical neck,
rim wide, everted, and fire-polished; irregular disc
base; thread handles with curl at upper attachment.
Amber glass with green iridescence; handles blue;
relief decoration consists of vertical ribs, above and
below a central horizontal band of running spirals,
between double horizontal bands; vertical mold joints.
Parallels: Avigad 1980: figs. 95,96 (Jerusalem); Auth
1976: nos. 329, 330.

99. Beaker (NOT ILLUSTRATED)

Eastern Mediterranean
Early Roman Period, 1st cent. CE
Glass: possibly mold-blown
Ht. 9.5 cm., diam. 8.4 cm.
Purchased in New York, said to come from Nazareth
Gift of Dr. Harry G. Friedman, 1958   F 4558

This drinking cup was probably used for wine.
The Jewish custom in later Talmudic times
required that each person at a banquet retain his
own cup, as opposed to the Roman custom in
which one cup was passed from guest to guest
(Zevulun and Olenik 1978: 13).

Description: vertical-sided, slightly widening toward
bottom; two repoussé horizontal bands, near rim and
base; rim flares, fire-polished; base slightly concave.
Trace of punty mark. Pale green tinge, iridescence.
Parallels: Hayes 1975: no. 139.

100.   Earring

Eastern Mediterranean
Probably Roman Period, 50 BCE–300 CE
Gold: hammered and drawn wire
Width 1.6 cm., length 1.4 cm.
Purchased in Israel
Gift of the Betty and Max Ratner Collection   1981–210

The rounded crescent or boat-shaped earring is a
common style beginning in the Bronze Age and
may have developed from a Sumerian style
(*Swedish Cyprus Expedition IV, pt. 2:* 385). The
prevailing style in the Bronze Age through the
Hellenistic Period seems to consist of an unclosed
hook or simple hook-and-loop closure, which
allowed the earring to be easily removed. In this
earring, however, the closing wires are twisted
securely around each other. The earring was
therefore probably meant to be left on the ear
for extended periods of time. This "permanent"
boat-shaped ring seems more common in Roman
times.

Description: hollow, rounded crescent, narrowing to
solid wires at ends which are twisted around each
other; body made by turning a flat sheet of gold; seam
is visible along exterior of ring.
Bibliography: Kozloff 1978: no. RC 169, color pl. 6.
Parallels: Culican 1973: pl. I:D (Tharros, Sardinia), III:
E,F,G, IV:B (Malta), C (Carthage); Harding 1951: pl. IX:35
(Amman tomb); *Swedish Cyprus Expedition IV, pt. 2:*
fig. 26:2a,b, fig. 31:2a,b, fig. 34:2a,b,c.

100

101. Pendant

Eastern Mediterranean
Probably Roman Period, 1st cent. BCE–4th cent. CE
Gold: hammered, braided, granulated; opal (?) and
  pearl: drilled
Length 8.5 cm.
Purchased in Israel
Gift of the Betty and Max Ratner Collection   1981–99

This pendant probably once hung from a
necklace or diadem; the multiple loops at the top
seem to have allowed for its attachment to more
than one chain, rather than a single ear wire.

Description: four-sided plaited chain with cubic
finials on each end; each cube has molded ridge at top
and bottom, seam visible; loop attached to each cube;
through top loop are a single ring and waisted ring
with flattened ends (probably bent out of original
shape); suspended from loop on bottom is a composite
pendant: a looped wire on top with granule, a gold ball
attached to carinated gold pear drop; on vertical wire
are pearl and oval opal (?) stone with convex face and
flat back; wire is curled on bottom to hold stone.
Bibliography: Kozloff 1978: no. RC 58, color pl. 6.
Parallels: Brilliant 1979: 133, pl. 59 (Pompeii), Higgins
1961: pl. 44 (Tarquinia), pl. 55a (Beaurains).

102. Earring

Eastern Mediterranean
Hellenistic–Roman Periods, 2nd cent. BCE–4th cent. CE
Gold: wire and bead; stone (emerald?): polished and
  drilled
Length 2.9 cm.
Purchased in Israel
Gift of the Betty and Max Ratner Collection   1981–100

Description: ear wire in oval loop, hook on one end
and closure loop on other; second wire runs through
gold bead and emerald, with twisted bottom; top
ending in loop which hangs from ear wire; pretzel-
shaped wire is attached to this second wire above the
stones and bead.
Bibliography: Kozloff 1978: no. RC 59, color pl. 6.
Parallels: Brilliant n.d.: 156,157 (on frescoes, Pompeii).

101

102

103. Oil Lamp

Israel
Early Roman Period, 50 BCE–1st cent. CE
Clay: wheel-turned body, applied nozzle, knife-
    trimmed, slipped, fired
Ht. 3 cm., length 9.I cm.
Provenance unknown
JM 14–69

These wheel-made lamps continue the tradition of the early closed lamps of the Late Hellenistic Period (see no. 74). The fan-like shape of the nozzle is a variation developed in Israel. This type of lamp, when undecorated, has been called Herodian, since it was believed to have originated around the beginning of the reign of Herod the Great over Judah (37–4 BCE). However, an excavated house in the Jewish Quarter of Jerusalem, whose destruction has been dated by the excavator to the end of Herod's reign, has yielded several types of 1st century BCE lamps but no "Herodian" ones (Avigad 1980: 88). It is thus possible that archaeologists will have to alter their dating of the appearance of this lamp form.

Description: convex-sided body; fill hole in center of top with ridge recessed from but encircling the hole; fan-shaped nozzle. Red ware; white slip.
Parallels: *Ramat Rahel II:* fig. 10:23; Mazar 1971: 33:33 (Jerusalem); Rahmani 1961: fig. 5:24,25 (Jerusalem tombs); Avigad 1980: pl. 58:3 (Jerusalem); *Masada:* 148; Bar Adon 1977: fig. 15:20 (En el-Ghuweir).

104. Oil Lamp

Italy
Late Roman Period, 4th cent. CE
Clay: mold-formed, slipped, fired
Ht. 3.1 cm., diam. 7.1
Purchased in Israel
Gift of the Betty and Max Ratner Collection   1981–91

These round lamps with short nozzles began to be imported into Israel from Italy in the second half of the 1st century CE. They were used side by side with the mold-made, decorated version of the "Herodian" lamp (see no. 137), although they never gained as much popularity (Kahane 1961: 130). The taller body, upright handle, and sharp carination on this lamp in the Jewish Museum collection date it late in the series, but it represents a continuation of the earlier type, on which gladiator fights were popular decorative motifs.

Description: straight, diverging sides of body meet upper half with an incision around body at the join; shoulder has sunken discus in center surrounded by two incised concentric circles, outer part slopes downward to meet body; small, off-center fill hole in disc; short, round nozzle, flat on top; vertical disc handle with rib running to base; base flat, surrounded by an incised circle. Discus decorated in relief with two helmeted gladiators in combat, one standing with shield and sword, the other on one knee with sword upraised, both on a ground line. Orange-pink ware, buff slip.
Bibliography: Kozloff 1978: no. RC 98, figs. 51,52.
Parallels: *Corinth IV:* pls. 10,27; Baur 1922: fig. 117:639.

103

104

105. Weight (NOT ILLUSTRATED)

Israel
Early–Middle Roman Period, late 1st cent. BCE–
  2nd cent. CE
Limestone: ground
Ht. 2.6 cm., diam. 4.25 cm., wt. 78.8 gms.
Purchased in Israel
Gift of the Betty and Max Ratner Collection
  1981–116

Cylindrical weights of hard limestone were
introduced into Israel during the Roman Period.
While those used in Italy had graded values,
archaeologists have been unable to reconstruct a
set of standard values for the weights used in the
Levant. The Romans apparently adjusted their
standards to those of local merchants. Many are
marked with the letters "LIB," Latin "LIBRA" or
pound, but their actual weights vary greatly from
one area to another. Some weights also bear a
letter standing for a year in the reign of a
particular ruler.

Description: low cylinder with illegible marks on one
of the flat surfaces.
Bibliography: Kozloff 1978: no. RC 74.
Parallels: Mazar 1969: pl. 11:12,13,14 (Jerusalem);
Avigad 1980: fig. 127 (Jerusalem); de Vaux 1959: pl.
12b (Feshka); Mazar 1971: pl. 23 (Jerusalem).

106. Wide Mouth Juglet (Cup?)

Probably Israel
Hasmonean or Early Roman Period, 3rd cent. BCE–1st
  cent. CE
Clay: wheel turned, handle pulled, slipped, fired
Ht. 8.4 cm., diam. 9.7 cm.
Purchased in Israel, 1981
Gift of the Betty and Max Ratner Collection   1982–3

The shape of this vessel is reminiscent of clay
and bronze forms found in Greece during the
4th–3rd centuries BCE. Vessels of this type have
been called drinking or cooking cups. They may
have been used to hold or boil hot drinks; we
know that in Talmudic times the wine was
diluted with hot or cold water (Zevulun and
Olenik 1979: 19).

Description: biconical body; bowl-like mouth (with
convex sides), rim vertical with rounded edge;
constriction at join of neck and body; handle with oval
cross-section; bottom comes to a blunt point. Pink
ware; black slip on upper third of vessel, white slip on
lower two-thirds.
Parallels: Avigad 1980: 211 (Jerusalem); Rahmani
1961: pl. VII:3 (Jerusalem tombs); Netzer 1977: fig. 8
(Jericho); *Ashdod I:* pl. VII:7.

107. Bowl

Israel
Hasmonean–Early Roman Period, mid-2nd cent. BCE–
  mid-1st cent. CE
Clay: wheel-turned, slipped, fired
Ht. 5.4 cm., diam. 11.2 cm.
Purchased in Israel
Gift of the Betty and Max Ratner Collection
  1981–164

Description: straight-sided body, diverging toward
rim, with low carination; internal groove at carination
point; rim straight-sided, slightly flaring; low ring base
placed too high above bowl bottom, so bowl actually
rests on its curved bottom and not on the base. Buff
ware; buff-white slip, slightly greenish slip on rim.
Parallels: Lapp 1968: fig. 17:20 (Beth Zur).

106

107

108. Spouted Cup

Israel
Early–Middle Roman Period, 50 BCE–150 CE
Limestone: chiseled and lathe-turned
Ht. 7 cm., diam. 6 cm.
Purchased in Israel
Gift of the Betty and Max Ratner Collection   1981–55

Limestone vessels with one or two handles and a spout are fairly common in Palestine during the Early and Middle Roman Periods. They have been called "measuring cups" because they come in a large range of sizes, although it has not yet been established if the sizes are standard. They could not have been used for liquid measures since limestone is absorptive; they may have been used for dry measures.

Description: barrel-shaped; flat bottom; vertical chisel marks on exterior, lathe-smoothed; flat rectangular vertical handle with large circular perforation; small spout extends from rim, completely reconstructed.
Bibliography: Kozloff 1978: no. RC 41.
Parallels: *Ramat Rahel II:* pl. 8:3; Avigad 1980: fig. 209:1, fig. 141 (Jerusalem); Rahmani 1961: fig. 5:26 (Jerusalem tombs); Yadin 1965: pl. 24:b (Masada); *de Vaux 1953:* fig 3:12 (Khirbet Qumran).

109

Eastern Sigillata Ware

During the Early Roman Period (1st cent. BCE), a glossy red-slipped pottery called Eastern Sigillata ware began to appear in Israel. It is believed to be a local imitation of the very fine mold-made Samian or Arretine ware produced as luxury items during the Roman Period in Italy and Gaul, some of which also found its way to Israel (Avigad 1980: 88). The term "sigillata" means "stamped" and generally signifies that the vessel bears a potter's stamp; sometimes the term "sigliata" is used, which means "initialed." Frequently, the local imitations do not bear a stamp.

It is generally agreed that there are several types of Eastern Sigillata ware, which can be classified regionally by the color of their fabric and slip. However, no clear typology has yet been established.

109. Eastern Sigillata Ware Bowl

Israel
Early Roman Period, 1st cent. BCE–1st cent. CE
Clay: wheel-turned, slipped, fired
Ht. 6.6 cm., diam. 12.8 cm.
Purchased in Israel, 1981
Gift of the Betty and Max Ratner Collection   1982–17

Description: convex-sided body diverging slightly toward rim; straight rim with slightly thickened exterior; cylindrical base, lower portion with molded exterior; bottom of base concave with its sides slanting on diagonal toward center of bowl bottom. Buff ware; red slip (quite thin in some areas).
Parallels: *Samaria-Sebaste III:* fig. 65:2; *Nessena I:* pl. 44:G; Avigad 1980: fig. 230 (Jerusalem).

108

110

110. Eastern Sigillata Ware Jug

Eastern Mediterranean
Late Hellenistic–Early Roman Period, 2nd–1st cent.
  BCE
Clay: wheel-turned, handle rolled, slipped, burnished,
  fired
Ht. 19.5 cm., diam. 19.5 cm.
Provenance unknown
Loaned by the Yale University Art Gallery
Gift of Rebecca Darlington Stoddard   1913.509

The form of this jug imitates a Greek prototype
(the *lagynos*) of the 4th–2nd centuries BCE.
However, it is made of the lustrous, red-slipped
Eastern Sigillata ware of the Early Roman Period.
A similar but larger jug of this carinated shape
was found in the wall niche of an Early Roman

Period home in the Jewish Quarter of Jerusalem.
The excavator has suggested that this cupboard,
which had slots for a shelf and was filled with
pottery, was used for the storage and display of
the household wares (Avigad 1980: 86). This jug
was probably used to serve wine.

Description: convex-sided body with horizontal
shoulder and sharp carination at join with body;
cylindrical neck narrows toward rim; flaring rim with
flat surface; handle made of four vertical rolls of clay,
with carinated angle; ring base; two grooves on neck
between handle and rim. Red ware; red lustrous slip.
Bibliography: Baur 1922: fig. 47:509.
Parallels: Avigad 1980: pl. 230 (Jerusalem); Lapp
1961: Type 228.A (Samaria-Sebaste); Thompson 1934:
fig. 92:E72.

111. Piriform Bottle

Israel
Early Roman Period, ca. 20 BCE–70 CE
Clay: wheel-turned, slipped, fired
Ht. 13.7 cm., diam. 5.7 cm.
Provenance unknown
JM 7–69

These pear-shaped bottles are quite common in the tombs of Israel during the 1st century BCE–1st century CE and seem to replace the spindle bottles for tomb use during the course of the 1st century BCE. They may have held oils or scents.

However, their discovery in occupation levels, such as in the houses of the Jewish Quarter in Jerusalem and especially in the wall cupboard, suggests they contained commodities for home use as well.

Description: piriform body; cylindrical neck with slight bulge at midpoint; rim flares outward and down; base flat. Pink-red ware; dark red slip.
Parallels: Rahmani 1980: pl. VII:1–4 (Mt. Scopus tombs); *Tell en-Nasbeh II:* pl. 75:1735; Mazar 1971: 33:30 (Jerusalem); Avigad 1980: fig. 124 (Jerusalem); de Vaux 1953: fig. 3:10 (Khirbet Qumran).

112. Piriform Bottle

Israel
Early Roman Period, 20 BCE–70 CE
Clay: wheel-turned, slipped, fired
Ht. 11.8 cm., diam. 4.9 cm.
Purchased in Israel
Gift of the Betty and Max Ratner Collection
1981–138

Description: piriform body, slightly lopsided; cylindrical neck, twisted; rim flares with exterior rolled thickening; disc base. Light red ware; brown slip.
Bibliography: Kozloff 1978: no. RC 96.
Parallels: See no. 111.

112   111

113. Cooking Pot

Israel
Early–Middle Roman Period, 1st cent. BCE–2nd
 cent. CE
Clay: wheel-turned, pulled handles, fired
Ht. 17.3 cm., diam. 20.2
Purchased in Israel
Gift of the Betty and Max Ratner Collection   1981–93

The basic form of the cooking pot, with its globular body, wide mouth, and two handles, remains unchanged from the Iron Age (see nos. 9, 14, 15). Various stylistic indicators, such as the horizontal ribbing and minor alterations in shape, can help archaeologists date these pots more closely.

Description: slightly compressed globular body, gently carinated at midpoint and near bottom; spiral ribbing on body; cylindrical neck, flares to join body; rim flared, exterior ridge below rim; slightly pointed bottom; handles have flat oval cross-section with wide, shallow groove down center. Red ware.
Bibliography: Kozloff 1978: no. RC 50, fig. 68.
Parallels: Mazar and Dothan 1966: fig. 26:12,13 (Tell Goren); *Ramat Rahel I*: fig. 6:20; Avigad 1980: fig. 111.

113

114

115

114. Juglet

Israel
Hasmonean–Early Roman Period, 2nd–1st cent. BCE
Clay: wheel-turned, pulled handle, slipped, fired
Ht. 13 cm., diam. 8.2 cm.
Purchased in Israel, 1981
Gift of the Betty and Max Ratner Collection   1982–1

Description: globular body with slight horizontal ribbing; thin cylindrical neck; rim, strongly inverted with carinated exterior ridge, forms cup-like mouth; bottom round; handle slightly twisted, cross-section oval. Pink ware; buff slip.
Parallels: *Ramat Rahel I:* fig. 6:16,17; *Ramat Rahel II:* fig. 10:14–17, fig. 28:4; Bar Adon 1977: fig. 12:1–5, 16–22 (En el-Ghuweir); Lapp and Lapp 1958: fig. 1:3, fig. 2:3 (Beth Zur); Mazar 1971: 33:25, pl. XXII:15–17 (Jerusalem).

115. Juglet

Israel
Possibly Middle–Late Roman Period, 1st–4th cent. CE
Clay: wheel-turned, pulled handle, fired
Ht. 8.4 cm., diam. 6.2 cm.
Purchased in Israel, 1981
Gift of the Betty and Max Ratner Collection   1982–2

Description: globular body; concave-sided neck flares out to rim with carinated ridge at the join; rim vertical interior and exterior; handle slightly twisted with convex underside and flat upper surface; disc base. Orange-pink ware.
Parallels: *Bethany:* pl. 128:a11,b4,12,13; Lapp 1961: Type 31.2A-S.

116

116. Shekel

Tyre, Lebanon
Early Roman Period, 45/46 CE
Silver: cast and stamped
Diam. 2.5 cm., wt. 14.2 grns.
Purchased in Israel
Gift of the Betty and Max Ratner Collection 1981 190

Reverse inscription in Greek:

ΤΥΡΟΥΙΕ [ΡΑΣ ΚΑΙ] ΑΕΥΛΟΥ/ΡΟΑ ΚΡ

Tyre the Holy [and city of Shelter]. Year 171 [of the Tyre era].

The silver shekels produced in Tyre, Lebanon, were the only coins permissible for payments to the Temple in Jerusalem. Despite their pagan symbolism, illustrated here by the head of the Phoenician god Melqart/Herakles and the Roman imperial eagle, the standardized quality and weight of the Tyrian shekels made them the most reliable for Temple use. Jewish law required a tax of one didrachma for every Jew in the world for the Temple, and a surcharge was levied if it was not paid in the Tyrian currency (Jeremias 1969: 26).

Description: obverse: head of Melqart/Herakles; reverse: eagle and sheaves of grain, Greek inscription. Score mark across eagle's neck possibly for testing silver in antiquity.
Bibliography: Kozloff 1978: no. RC 149.
Parallels: Meshorer (forthcoming): no. 30.

117. Six-wick Oil Lamp

Southern Israel
Byzantine, 4th–5th cent. CE
Clay: mold-made, rolled handle, fired
Length 12.2 cm., width 8.8 cm.
Provenance unknown
Gift of Dr. Harry G. Friedman   S 946

Lamps of this shape with from three to eight wick holes in a row across the front are found in the tombs of Judah (*Tell en-Nasbeh I:* 61–62). Since one-wick lamps are still being produced at this time, the significance of the multiple wicks is unknown (see discussion in no. 132).

The gabled structure on this lamp is intended to represent the Torah ark from a synagogue, with the interior archway symbolizing the scallop-shaped niche within the ark. Similar architectural representations of this motif are found in the early synagogues, e.g., painted above a similarly shaped Torah ark niche at Dura-Europos (*Goodenough III:* fig. 602). The amphora in the center is probably meant to symbolize the wine used in Jewish ritual, since other lamps bear representations of similarly shaped amphorae between two grape bunches.

Description: flat body, square on the wick end with round back; heavy seam where upper and lower molded halves are joined; central fill-hole surrounded by two double-ridged raised rings; six wick holes; very low ring base; strap handle with round dot of clay at upper end. Decoration on flat top in raised relief depicts two twisted columns supporting a gabled roof, two smaller interior columns joined by a twisted "rope" arch, and a two-handled pedestaled jug in the center of the arch; three center-dot circles and one concentric center-dot circle on either side of gable; beaded border. Pink ware, fire-blackened upper surface.
Bibliography: *Goodenough III:* fig. 287.
Parallels: *Goodenough III:* fig. 286 (Bittur), fig. 289 (Tell en-Nasbeh); Sussman 1972:25; *Bethany:* fig. 17; *Tell en-Nasbeh I:* pl. 73:1678.

118. Jug, possibly Terra Sigillata Ware

Israel
Early Roman Period, 1st cent. BCE
Clay: wheel-turned, rolled handle, slipped, fired
Ht. 20.8 cm., diam 18.2 cm.
Provenance unknown
JM 9–69

This one-handled jug was probably a decanting vessel for wine, as can be seen on Roman reliefs and mosaic floors and on a representation of a serving table on a table top from Jerusalem (Zevulun and Olenik 1979: nos. 57,58,59). This type of vessel may have been used to pour out the wine libation in the Temple, although it would have been made of silver or gold (Num. 7:13). Wine was offered by the priests twice a day at the Temple as part of the daily service, and also accompanied the burnt and peace offerings (Num. 15:1–10).

Description: globular body; cylindrical neck, slightly concave-sided; wide everted rim with flat top slanting diagonally inward to neck; wide flat handle with groove down center; ring base with small stamped circle with raised center. Light orange ware; red slip.
Parallels: Baur 1922: fig. 47:510; Thompson 1934: fig. 63.

117

118

119

119. Incense Shovel

Eastern Mediterranean
Early–Middle Roman Period, 1st–2nd cent. CE
Bronze: cast
Length 30 cm., width 12.2 cm.
Purchased in Jerusalem
JM 5-69

Among the furnishings of the Temple mentioned
in the Bible are objects which may illuminate the
function of the shovel represented here. These
are the shovels, fire pans, and censers used in
the service of the altar (Ex. 27:3, 38:3, Lev. 16:12).
The shovel was used to carry coals from the
sacrificial altar to the incense altar in front of the
Holy of Holies. The offering of incense was made
each morning and evening and also accompanied
offerings of meal, of the first fruits on *Shavuot,*
and was displayed in the Temple with the
showbread.

Archaeologists have found actual ancient shovels,
possessing two flat cups in the corners of the
pan, and have identified them as incense and
perfume burners. Since these have been found in
the Italian sites of Pompeii and Herculaneum, as
well as in Israel, archaeologists have connected
them with pagan ritual. However, there was a
tradition of the use of the shovels both in Temple
ritual and as representations in post-destruction
art, usually associated with Temple furnishings
like the *menorah.* There seems to be no cogent
reason, therefore, for denying a Jewish use for
this shovel. Since all sacrificial activity was
forbidden when the Temple was destroyed in 70
CE, the burning of incense afterwards may not
have been cultic, but merely for its pleasing odor.

Description: rectangular pan with everted ledge rim
decorated with two incised grooves and resting on four
knobbed feet; handle with round cross-section, grooved
on underside, decorated with stylized vegetation motif;
leaf terminal on handle with lion foot as support; two
conical-shaped hollows added on corners of pan were
meant to receive the base of flat cups that would have
held the incense. The cups and the bridge between
them (which would have held them in place) are
missing.
Parallels: Yadin 1961: 39, pl. 20B (Cave of the
Letters); *Goodenough III:* fig. 439 (Dura-Europos);
Richter 1915: fig. 658.

120. Mortar and Pestle

Israel
Early Roman Period, 50 BCE–70 CE
Basalt: ground and incised
Ht. 11 cm., width 25 cm.
Purchased in Israel, 1981
Gift of the Betty and Max Ratner Collection   1982–24

Similar grinding stones have been found in the Early Roman Period houses in the upper city of Jerusalem. They were ordinary domestic implements, used to grind the flour for the daily bread. However, it is also likely that they produced the flour for certain special offerings that were brought to the Temple during the three annual holy-day pilgrimages to Jerusalem. For instance, the first fruit offering on *Shavuot* was made from "corn in the ear parched with fire, even groats of the fresh ear" (Lev. 2:14), and was made into cakes containing leavening and honey that were brought to the sanctuary. One of the three basic types of offerings made on the altar twice daily and on holy days by the priests, and also on behalf of individuals for special reasons, was a meal made of fine flour, oil, and frankincense. This flour, too, would have been ground on a mortar such as the one discussed here, as well as the flour for the Passover *matzah*.

Description: Square top with circular central depression, quite smooth from use, incised circle around depression; four rectangular protrusions on the corners, each incised with three parallel lines radiating outward from the bowl; three legs with hemispherical cross-section flat side outward. Pestle: truncated cone.
Parallels: Avigad 1980: figs. 123,209:4 (Jerusalem); *Samaria-Sebaste III:* fig. 117:7; *Ashdod I:* fig. 1:10.

121. Piriform Bottle

Eastern Mediterranean
Early Roman Period, 1st cent. CE
Glass: free-blown and banded
Ht. 12.3 cm., diam. 7.4 cm.
Purchased in New York
Gift of Elaine and Harvey Rothenberg   1979–97

This bottle, although probably not the type used in the ritual service, is a common container for oil and perfume in the Roman Period. This is indicated by the chemical analysis of the intact contents of two glass "unguentaria" from the 2nd–3rd centuries which proved to be filled with olive oil (Barag 1972; Basch 1972). Olive oil was an essential element of the offerings made by individuals at the Temple, where it was mixed with the ground meal and then burned. Although we cannot know for sure, one can imagine that bottles such as this contained small amounts of oil that may have been purchased near the Temple by worshippers as part of their offering.

Description: piriform body with slight "waist;" cylindrical neck constricted at base, rim flat and everted, folded out and over; base flat with crescent-shaped depression. Light green glass, surface decoration of white thread in swirl pattern.
Parallels: *Ashdod II–III:* 205, fig. 105:9 (pl. 98:11); *Samaria-Sebaste III:* 412:11, fig. 95:11 (redated in *Ashdod II–III:* 205).

120

121

122

122. Ossuary

Israel
Early Roman Period, 1st cent. BCE–1st cent. CE
Limestone: chiseled and incised
Ht 28 cm., length 53.8 cm., depth 22.8 cm.
Purchased in Israel
Gift of the Betty and Max Ratner Collection
1981–101

The custom of burial in rock-hewn communal tombs (probably organized by families) is continuous in Israel from the Iron Age to the Second Temple Period. A new feature of the tradition is the cutting of long narrow niches off a central passage in which the deceased were placed, instead of on open benches. Vessels containing offerings of food and oil, and lamps were placed in the niches or in front of their plastered seals, similar to Iron Age practice. Recent evidence from rock-cut tombs in Jericho has suggested that a transition in Jewish burial practice occurred at the end of the 1st century BCE, from primary burial in wooden coffins to secondary burial in small limestone caskets or ossuaries, such as the one depicted here. The practice of secondary burial is best described through the words of a later Talmudic source: "A man gathers the bones of his father and mother for it is a joy unto him. At first they would bury in pits. [When] the flesh was eaten, they would gather the bones and bury them in chests" (Jerus. Talmud, *Moed Katan* 1:5 [80c]).

Some scholars see a long continuum of secondary burial in ancient Israel from the 4th millennium on, reflected in the care with which the bones in communal tomb burials were piled to make room for new burials (Meyers 1971: 3–11). Others suggest that ossuary burial signified a shift to belief in resurrection of the body (Rahmani 1961: 117), a belief already known in Israel in the 2nd century BCE (Macc. 7:10–11, 12:43–45, 14:46). Another interpretation of ossuary burial is that it signified a belief in expiation of one's sins after the flesh had decayed (Hachlili 1980: 239, Meyers 1971: 95). The ossuary in the Jewish Museum collection bears the typical carved decoration of rosettes, common during the Early Roman Period. The rosette symbol has an eastern (i.e., Mesopotamian or Persian) origin (Meyers 1971: 47), although its meaning in this context is unknown. This ossuary was meant to have a gabled lid which is now missing.

Description: rectangular box with four low feet. Decoration on one long face only: two rosettes, each surrounded by a scalloped border, then by a wave pattern bordered by two lines; two rows of the wave pattern border three sides of the face, with one row on bottom; two vertical rows also separate the rosettes. Traces of orange may be remains of paint.
Bibliography: Kozloff 1978: no. RC 60, fig. 48.
Parallels: Hachlili 1980: 238 (Jericho tombs); Rahmani 1961: pl. 14:3,4 pl. 16:1 (Jerusalem Tombs).

Epilogue: Early Synagogues and the Development of Jewish Symbols

The Roman destruction of the Temple in Jerusalem in 70 CE and the dispersion of Jews from the city radically altered the form of Jewish worship. The loss of the spiritual and geographical focus of the religion forced the Jews to turn to a secondary religious institution, the synagogue, which had probably existed contemporaneously with the Temple for several centuries. The synagogue replaced and expanded three religious functions of the Temple, becoming a house of prayer, of assembly and of learning.

One of the most profound changes in Jewish worship was the geographical shift of its focus away from Jerusalem and toward the local community synagogues which sprang up throughout the Mediterranean and parts of Europe. Jerusalem remained, throughout the Diaspora, the spiritual center for Judaism, the object of pilgrimages, the most honored burial place for a Jew, and the focus of hopes for the rebuilding of the Temple. However, the performance of the ritual was now centered in individual communities; Jews no longer made the three annual pilgrimages to the Temple on *Pesach, Shavuot* and *Sukkot.* In time, the synagogue became not only the center for prayer and learning, but also a communal social center, thereby taking on the role of the most important Jewish institution.

A number of major changes occurred in the form of Jewish worship. Chief among them was the prohibition of all types of sacrificial offerings, since sacrifice, particularly of animals, had been the prerogative of the Temple in Jerusalem. Offerings of wine, meal and incense had been allowed in the two known Diaspora temples of Delos and Elephantine before the destruction, but animal sacrifice had always been limited to the Jerusalem Temple. With the cessation of sacrifice, the use of the ritualistic implements accompanying its performance was discontinued. Archaeologists do not find altars, incense stands or shovels, or vessels of any type in the synagogues. The new focus of worship consisted of prayer and perhaps the reading of the Hebrew Scriptures.

The second major change in Jewish ritual was the inclusion of the worshipper in most phases of its performance inside the religious structure. When the Temple still functioned, the sacrificial rituals were performed daily by the priesthood in the interior of the building; worshippers did not witness them and were only allowed in the Temple courtyard.

The destruction of the Temple also resulted in the dissolution of the priesthood system which serviced it. The hierarchical and hereditary organization of the Temple priests was superceded by the community teachers, the rabbis, who studied and interpreted the Jewish laws for the populace.

The synagogue form of worship in use today has its roots in the first century CE, if not earlier. Scholars disagree on when the first type of non-sacrificial Jewish worship originated, but all agree that some form of it existed before the destruction of the Temple. Most propose that the Babylonian Exile produced the first true synagogue, for it seemed logical that the Exiles would have met to read the Torah. However, the earliest archaeologically attested synagogue is found at Delos in Greece, dating to the early first century BCE. In Israel, the bench-lined assembly halls found at the Herodian fortresses of Masada and Herodium have been interpreted as synagogues dating to the late first century CE. No recognizable synagogues have been found in Israel from the period between the first and third centuries CE; if they existed, they were probably architecturally indistinct from domestic rooms. Beginning in the third century CE, synagogues became quite numerous in Israel as well as in the Diaspora

The general plan of the synagogues was a columned hall lined with benches for the worshippers. No Torah arks have been found in synagogues from the first and second centuries CE, and it has been assumed that they were movable wooden structures which have since disintegrated. However, around the third century CE, permanent niches with pediments and columned facades have been found at Nabratein in the Galilee (Meyers, Strange and Meyers 1981) and at Dura-Europos in Syria (Kraeling 1956). The earliest synagogues were undecorated, but around the third century CE mosaic floors with geometric designs began to appear in synagogues and churches, much like those in Herodian houses in Jerusalem of the first century CE. By the fourth century CE, the long-standing rabbinic injunction against using graven images seems to have been lifted, and all forms of human, mythological and animal decorations appear in mosaic floors, wall frescos and ceilings (cf. nos. 123–126). While some of the decorative elements were borrowed from Roman art (although apparently without their pagan symbolism), strictly Jewish themes were also represented.

The post-destruction period also witnessed the great proliferation of Jewish symbols in art, many of which still have meaning today. Chief among them was the seven-branched *menorah* which had been an important implement of the Temple in Jerusalem.

One of these *menorot* was carried off to Rome by the destroyers of the Temple, as is depicted in the triumphal procession on the Arch of Titus in Rome. According to the Talmud, it was forbidden to make exact copies of the Temple *menorah* in metal, and this prohibition is largely observed even today. This did not prevent its depiction in art (cf. nos. 127,130,131,135,136). After the destruction of the Temple, the *menorah* appears to have become the emblem of Judaism throughout the millennia, and was adopted as the official symbol of the State of Israel.

Frequently accompanying the *menorah* are representations of two other ritual implements used in the Temple: the incense shovel, probably used to carry coals and incense to be burned on the altar, and the ram's horn or *shofar*, which was blown on *Rosh Hashanah*, the New Year. Also reminiscent of the glory of the destroyed Temple is the depiction of the Torah ark

with two columns, pediment and arched niche for the scrolls. Two-handled storage jars often associated with these arks were probably meant to symbolize the sacrificial wine.

Objects which were brought to the Temple in Jerusalem during the three annual pilgrimages also appear frequently in Jewish art. The bundle of palm fronds, myrtle and willow sprigs (called the *lulav*), and the citron fruit (called the *etrog*) were brought to the Temple during the Feast of Tabernacles (*Sukkot*) and are still used today. Pomegranates and barley were two of the seven species brought as a first fruit offering on the Spring holiday of *Shavout*, the Feast of Weeks (cf. nos. 123–125).

The illustration of biblical scenes begins to appear in art in the Late Roman to Early Byzantine Periods both in mosaic synagogue pavements like that at Beth Alpha, and on oil lamps (cf. no. 133). The use of Bible stories as a subject of decoration is extremely popular in much later Jewish ceremonial art and Christian minor arts from Europe.

The 1st to 2nd centuries after the destruction of the Temple marked a turning point in the history of the Jewish religion. The centralized religion developed under King Solomon, revolving around sacrificial rites at the Temple, was transformed into a local, community-based form of worship revolving around the Torah and its interpretation. The symbols and ritual objects primarily associated with the Temple became symbolic of the Temple after its destruction. These symbols were adopted by the Diaspora communities throughout the world and in some cases became the inspiration for synagogue decoration and ritual objects. Although these communities soon became isolated from each other and developed their own stylistic variations of the same objects and symbols (often based on the stylistic milieu of the host cultures), and their own adaptations of the ritual, the basic threads of the religion are still common to all. Thus, the symbols on objects from these early times were passed from generation to generation and are still vital today.

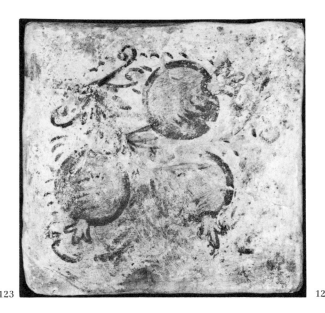

123

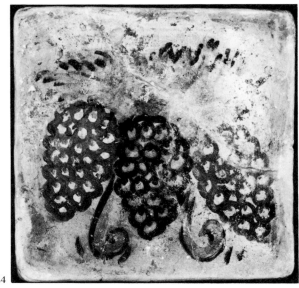

124

123. Ceiling Tile from a Synagogue

Dura-Europos, House of Assembly (Syria),
Middle Roman Period, before 256 CE
Clay: painted and fired
Length 38.3 cm., width 39 cm., depth 4.5 cm.
Loaned by the Yale University Art Gallery, Yale-French
 Excavations at Dura-Europos   1933.278

One of the best-known early Diaspora synagogues
is that at Dura-Europos in Syria; it consisted of a
dwelling (possibly for guests or for a staff
member), a forecourt, and a House of Assembly.
The latter was decorated with wall paintings, and
on the ceiling were some 500 painted clay tiles
mounted in plaster between wooden joists. Only
234 of the projected 500 were found by the
excavators, and three of these are on view (nos.
123–125). The decorative motifs used have both
pagan and Jewish significance.

The pomegranate depicted on this ceiling tile has
a long history of decorative use in Israel,
beginning at least in the Late Bronze Age (1550–
1200 BCE) with some pomegranate-finial "wands"
from Lachish (*Lachish II:* pl. 20:25,26). The
pomegranate is mentioned in the Bible as one of
the decorative elements on the priest's robe (Ex.
28:34) and it was one of the seven species
brought to the Temple with the first fruits on the
holiday of *Shavuot*. It appears both on the coins
of the Hasmoneans and on those produced
during the First Revolt against Rome. In this tile it
is perhaps merely the depiction of a fruit without
any symbolic significance; in other representations
such as the burial plaque no. 128 and lamp no.
137, it probably stands for the offerings that used
to be brought to the Temple.

Today, the Hebrew word for pomegranate,

rimmon, is used for the headpieces that cover the
wooden staves of the Torah roller. These
rimmonim are frequently shaped like globes on a
shaft, and it has been suggested that they
symbolize the fruit of the staves, which are called
in Hebrew *etz chayim,* the tree of life (Gutmann
1964: 15).

Description nearly square tile with painted
representation of three pomegranates with leaf and
scroll design. Colors: red, orange, black, and green.
Bibliography: *Dura-Europos VIII, pt. 1:* pl. 12:4.

124. Ceiling Tile from a Synagogue

Dura-Europos, House of Assembly (Syria)
Middle Roman Period, before 256 CE
Clay: painted and fired
Length 39 cm., width 39 cm., depth 5 cm.
Loaned by the Yale University Art Gallery, Yale-French
 Excavations at Dura-Europos   1933.280

The importance of grapes and wine was not
unique to the Jewish religion, for the ancient
Greeks and Romans poured libations of wine to
their gods, as did many other Near Eastern
cultures. Grapes were also a favorite secular
decorative element in the ancient world. The
grape bunches depicted on this tile are therefore
not necessarily meant as a Jewish symbol,
although numerous clay lamps of the 2nd–4th
centuries CE show grape bunches associated with
an amphora and a Torah ark, surely symbolic of
the sanctified wine used in the Temple (e.g.,
Sussman 1972: nos. 44,48,49).

Description: square plaque painted with design of
three bunches of grapes on a branch with vine
tendrils. Colors: pink, red, green, and black.
Bibliography: *Dura-Europos VIII, pt. 1:* pl. 13:2.

125. Ceiling Tile from a Synagogue (NOT ILLUSTRATED)

Dura-Europos, House of Assembly (Syria)
Middle Roman Period, before 256 CE
Clay: painted and fired
Length 38 cm., width 39 cm., depth 5 cm.
Loaned by the Yale University Art Gallery, Yale-French
 Excavations at Dura-Europos 1933.286

The heads of grain on this tile represent the staple food of most Near Eastern cultures. Here they could symbolize the ground meal and first fruit offerings that had been brought to the Temple in Jerusalem.

Description: square plaque, painted with design of three heads of grain among long, oval leaves. Colors: yellow and black.
Bibliography: *Dura-Europos VIII, pt. 1:* pl. 14:1.

126. Mosaic Floor Fragment

Israel
Early Byzantine Period, 4th–5th cent. CE
Stone: cut; mortar
Diam. 40 cm., size of tiles 1.4 × 1.4 × 0.9 cm.
Said to have been found in the Galilee
Gift of Erwin Harvith U 7529

Birds were commonly represented in the mosaic floors of the early synagogues and churches. The bird depicted here is probably a dove, identified by the bands on the neck and the striped tail. Similar birds were frequently depicted on either side of a tree or stand in the mosaics of Israel and North Africa. The bird on this mosaic is enclosed in a circle and was probably part of a composition of looped vines enclosing animals, a common decorative scheme in early Byzantine synagogues and churches.

Description: stone tiled roundel, depicting a bird with crown, banded neck, and striped wing and tail; above it is a lozenge form with a "tail." Bird has red beak, crown, band on neck and wing tip; rest of body is black and white; white eye with black center; beige feet; lozenge is black, red, pink, and white; background tiles are white, rim of roundel beige. Tiles and ancient mortar have been set in cement; traces of pitch around edges.
Parallels: Negev 1980: 219 (Maon Synagogue); Duval n.d.: fig. 15 (Kelibia, Tunisia).

126

Jewish Burial Plaques

Inscribed marble plaques with Jewish symbols on them are commonly found in European (primarily Italian) and Israeli catacombs. Long corridors and chambers were dug into the soft rock with rows of niches or "shelves" for the bodies of the deceased. After burial, the niche would be plastered over, and the marble dedicatory plaque embedded in the plaster. This form of interment was practiced by both Christians and Jews within the Roman Empire, differentiating them from the pagan Roman tradition of cremating the deceased and placing the ashes in funerary urns.

The Jewish community in Rome (the source of three of our burial plaques) is known from textual sources to have been in residence since at least the 1st century BCE (i.e., before the Diaspora). The digging of the underground catacombs has been interpreted as an adaptation of the millennia-long tradition in ancient Israel of using natural or artificially dug burial caves in cliff faces (Leon 1960: 54).

127. Burial Plaque

Rome, Vigna Randanini Catacomb on the Old Appian Way
Early-Middle Roman Period, 1st–3rd cent. CE
Marble: carved and painted
Ht. 29.5 cm., width 26.5 cm., depth 3 cm.
Gift of Henry L. Moses in memory of Mr. and Mrs. Henry P. Goldschmidt   JM 5–50

This burial plaque was photographed while still in the Vigna Randanini catacomb and published in 1936. It had come into the possession of a Zurich dealer from whom it was purchased and then donated to the Museum. The area inside the rectangle originally contained an inscription in red paint that is completely effaced today. In 1865, the original excavator of the tomb was able to discern a few Greek letters of the dedication, but these were insufficient to permit a complete translation (Garrucci 1865).

The plaque is richly decorated with Jewish symbols, most of which can be associated with Temple ritual objects or with festivals on which offerings were made at the Temple. The large central seven-branched *menorah* is depicted as a lampstand supporting seven oil lamps. To the left are an *etrog* (the citron symbolic of the fall holiday of *Sukkot*), below it a root vegetable (possibly the bitter herb used in the Passover feast) and a curved object probably representing *the shofar* or ram's horn blown on the New Year. To the right is an object which has been interpreted as a knife, symbolic of either circumcision or ritual sacrifice in the Temple, but which might easily be a profile view of the

incense shovel so frequently found with representations of Temple vessels. Below it is an amphora, probably symbolizing ritual wine or, less likely, oil, and the palm-frond bundle or *lulav* (also used during *Sukkot*). The rectangle above the *menorah* with the two triangles on either side, meant to hold the inscription, is a standard Roman name plate.

Bibliography: Garrucci 1865: no. 25; Vogelstein and Rieger 1896: no. 128; Frey 1975: no. 200; Leon 1960: 199,202,203, fig. 35; *Goodenough III:* fig. 769.

128. Burial Plaque

Rome, Vigna Randanini Catacomb on the Old Appian Way
Early-Middle Roman Period, 1st–3rd cent. CE
Marble: incised
Ht. 24.2 cm., width 25.3 cm., depth 2.2 cm.
Gift of Dr. Harry G. Friedman, 1958   F 4714

Inscription in Latin:
AEL[IA] ALEXANDRIA/AEL[IA] SEPTIMAE/ MATRI KARIS/ SIMAE BENE MER[EN]T[I] FECIT Ael[ia]
Alexandria set up [this stone] to Ael[ia] Septima, her dearest mother, in grateful memory.

This plaque was also still in place in the catacomb in 1936 when it was photographed and obtained through the same Zurich dealer as no. 127. The symbol on the left has been interpreted as an oil bottle, but would also seem to resemble a pomegranate, one of the first fruits taken to the Temple during the spring holiday of *Shavuot*. The ram in the center can symbolize one of several Jewish ceremonies, such as the blowing of the ram's horn on the New Year, or the animal sacrifices brought to the Temple. The object on the right is the *etrog* (citron).

Bibliography: Garrucci 1856: no. 1; Vogelstein and Rieger 1896: no. 140; Diehl 1927: no. 4967; Frey 1975 no. 208; Leon 1960: 202,293, fig. 56; *Goodenough III:* fig. 778.

129. Burial Plaque

Rome, Vigna Randanini Catacomb on the Old Appian Way
Early-Middle Roman Period, 1st–3rd cent. CE
Marble: incised
Ht. 28.2 cm., width 28.8 cm., depth 2.5 cm.
Gift of Dr. Harry G. Friedman   F 4715

Inscription in Latin:
AURELIA • PROTOGE/NIA • AUR[ELIAE] •
QUINTILLE/ MATRI KARISSIM[A]E/QU[A]E • VIXIT ANNIS •
LX M[ENSIBUS]V • B[ENE] • M[ERENTI] • POSUIT
Aurelia Protogenia set up [this stone] to Aur[elia] Quintilla, her dearest mother, who lived sixty years, 5 m[onths], in grateful memory

127

129

128

130

This plaque depicts the *lulav* and the *etrog*, the palm frond and citron still used during the fall festival of *Sukkot*. The representation of the *lulav* on the right is unusual and has been disputed because of the globular area in the center.

Bibliography: Garrucci 1865: no. 5; Vogelstein and Rieger 1896: no. 148; Diehl 1927: no. 4964; Frey 1975 no. 217; Leon 1960: 295, no. 217; *Goodenough III:* fig. 277.

130. Burial Plaque

Possibly Late Roman–Early Byzantine Period, 4th–5th cent.
Marble: incised
Ht. 24.1 cm., width 28.2 cm., depth 2.9 cm.
Latin inscription: HIC POSITUS EST FLAES EBREUS
　　　　　　　　Here lies Flaes the Jew.
Inscription in Hebrew: *Slm* [sic]
　　　　　　　　Pe[a]ce.
Purchased in Amsterdam, said to be from the neighborhood of Naples
Gift of Mr. Samuel Friedenberg in 1950　JM 3–50

This burial plaque has no known catacomb provenance, so we must rely on on analysis of its style and content for attribution. This particular form of the 7-branched *menorah* with tripod base and a bar across the lamps, combined with the addition of the Hebrew world *Shalom*, seems to be characteristic of the tombstones of the southern Italian city of Venosa. A Jewish catacomb was excavated there in the 1850's, belonging to a moderately sized Jewish community of the 4th–5th century CE (Frey 1975: 420–422; Leon 1954: 283–284). It is thus possible that this tombstone, said to be from around Naples, may have originated in the Venosa catacombs some 90 miles due east of Naples.

While the vast majority of Italian tombstones are exclusively inscribed in Latin or Greek, the addition of the Hebrew word for peace, *Shalom*, is occasionally found. The frequent misspellings of the word, as in this tombstone, has led scholars to suggest that the Italian Jews were not overly familiar with the Hebrew language. (Lifschitz 1975:24)

Bibliography: *Goodenough III:* fig. 893.
Parallels: Frey 1975: nos. 572,574,579,610,612,613,614.

131

131. Fragment of a Sarcophagus

Possibly Israel
Late Roman Period, 3rd–4th cent. CE
Marble: relief carved, incised, polished
Ht. 42 cm., length 55.6 cm., depth 6 cm.
Purchased in New York
Loaned by Daniel M. Friedenberg   L1982–3.3

This marble fragment was part of a sarcophagus rather than a plaque, for a small portion of the base is still preserved. Excavated representations of detailed *menorot* on sarcophagi are extremely rare in the ancient world; three are known from the Beth Shearim catacombs in Israel, and three from the catacombs in Rome (Avigad 1977: 108). A number of the features on this *menorah* are paralleled only in *menorah* representations on lamps found in Israel: the six arms, decorated with knobs, are curved and connected on top by a horizontal incised bar; the bottom arms rest on the tripod base, which has two curled legs ending

in knobs, and a triangular-shaped third leg. This particular way of representing the *menorah* base is not common, and the close parallel to the lamp representations suggests that the sarcophagus fragment may have come from Israel.

A number of fragments of marble sarcophagi and statuary, decorated in Roman style, were excavated at the Beth Shearim necropolis (Avigad 1977). Thus it is not unusual to find marble in Israel, although it was probably imported.

Description: fragment of long side and bottom corner of a sarcophagus with three surviving recessed panels. The first contains a seven-branched *menorah*, described above. The second, narrower panel contains a column with plain capital and fluted lower portion; the third panel survives in only one corner and the image does not appear. The angle at the bottom that joins side to base was broken away; interior and exterior have been polished.

Parallels: *Goodenough III:* figs. 334–337; Reifenberg 1936: figs. 9–11.

132. Seven-wick Oil Lamp

Southern Israel
Byzantine Period, 4th–5th cent. CE
Clay: mold-formed, rolled handle, fired
Length 13.3 cm., width 8.9 cm.
Ex-collection Garett, purchased in New York
Gift of Dr. Harry G. Friedman, 1951   F 2893

The form of this lamp, with its seven wicks in a row, is probably the prototype for 18th- and 19th-century CE stone, eight-wicked Hanukkah lamps made in Yemen, North Africa and France. Byzantine eight-wick lamps have been associated with Hanukkah lights, although lamps of this shape also come with any number of wick holes from three to eight.

The use of lamps with seven wicks, however, goes back to the 19th–17th centuries BCE in Syria, and the second half of the second millennium in Israel (C. Meyers 1976: 70; Smith 1964: 14). Archaeologists have interpreted them as cult objects, although they are found in houses and tombs as well as sanctuaries. The use of seven wicks, as in the seven-branched *menorah* of the Temple, probably had special significance in the Iron Age, and in the Byzantine Period as well.

The four columns represented on this lamp were possibly meant to symbolize the columns of the Temple of Jerusalem, or those of a synagogue. Representations of single columns or columns with arches also appear on much later Jewish ceremonial objects, such as marriage contracts and Torah curtains, while North African and Near Eastern Hanukkah lamps of the 18th–19th centuries CE are decorated with Moslem-style arches and architectural elements.

Description: flat body, square at wick end and round at back; two high and two low concentric ridges around fill hole; design on upper surface consists of four twisted columns on square bases, joined by beaded arches, with cross-hatch fill between the columns and center-dot circles in the corners; representation framed by beaded border. On base of nozzle a wavy line bisects the lamp, with seven lines running toward square end, and ending in scallops (forming a petal-like pattern); flat base has same pattern of rings as fill hole; thick join seam visible between upper and lower molds. Pink ware; white slip; fire-blackening on wick holes.

Bibliography: Kande, N.Y., Sale Catalogue no. 78.
Parallels: *Bethany:* fig. 17:7a; *Goodenough III:* figs. 273,275 (Gezer); *Tell en-Nasbeh I:* pl. 42:Tomb 33:19, fig. 23:11.

133. Oil Lamp

North Africa
Early Byzantine Period, 4th–5th cent. CE
Clay: mold-formed
Length 11.8 cm., width 6.9 cm.
Provenance unknown
Gift of Dr. Harry G. Friedman   F 4349

The representation of stories and events from the Hebrew Bible has been a common decorative element in both Jewish and Christian art for centuries. This lamp exemplifies the custom in its depiction of the return of the men sent by Moses from the wilderness into the land of Canaan to spy out the nature of the land and its inhabitants. They "came unto the valley of Eshcol, and cut down from thence a branch with one cluster of grapes, and they bore it on a pole between two; they took also of the pomegranates, and of the figs." (Num. 13:23). The twelve spies reported that the land of Canaan was indeed flowing with milk and honey, and showed as evidence the fruit they had brought.

Description: convex-sided bowl continues horizontally into spout; flat shoulder with two small fill holes; channel leads from shoulder to wick hole; fin-like vertical handle; disc base; rib from handle to base; faint circle stamped on base. Decoration on shoulder consists of the two spies standing frontally, carrying a bunch of grapes on a pole between them; around the scene are a row of concentric circles with interior lozenges with dots, alternating with squares filled with checkerboard pattern. Brown ware; black traces around nozzle and base of handle may be a slip, rather than fire-blackening.

Parallels: *Goodenough III:* fig. 933 (Syracuse), figs. 932,959 (Carthage); *Delos XXVI:* pl. 33:4690,4691,4693; Deneauve 1969: pl. 103:1138,1139,1134 (Carthage); Bailey 1980: no. Q1434.

133

134. Pilgrim Jug

Probably Jerusalem
Byzantine Period, late 6th–early 7th cent. CE
Glass: mold-blown, intaglio decoration, thread handle
Ht. 13.9 cm., width 8.7 cm.
Provenance unknown
Gift of Dr. Harry G. Friedman   F 4677

Scholars have long noticed a very homogenous group of hexagonal glass vessels in the form of squat jars or pitchers that bear either Jewish or Christian symbols on their six faces. Some of these vessels with identical decoration probably were made in the same mold. The accounts of Christian pilgrims to Jerusalem mention that they took oil from a lamp in the rock-cut tomb said to be that of Jesus, and the hexagonal bottles with Christian symbols may have been used by such pilgrims to transport this consecrated oil home. No such textual evidence exists for the interpretation of the vessels with Jewish symbols. It has been suggested that Jewish pilgrims followed the custom of taking oil from holy places or synagogues in Jerusalem, or used consecrated oil during the fasting and mourning for the destruction of the Temple on the 9th of Ab (Barag 1970:62). The custom would have ceased in 629 CE when the Jews were forbidden to enter Jerusalem. The intact condition of the surviving pilgrim vessels has led scholars to propose that they were placed in burials, perhaps to express a wish for resurrection or eternal life (Barag 1970: 54).

This vessel bears symbols that cannot be identified as either Jewish or Christian. The only recognizable representations are the amphora on face 1 and the lozenge on face 4, possibly depicting the ornate cover of a book. It has been recently suggested that the images on faces 3, 5, and 6 are human figures and possibly of Christian symbolism, but this identification is extremely tentative (Barag 1971: b 46-47). The lozenge and amphora are found in both the Christian and Jewish hexagonal vessels.

134

Description: hexagonal body, round shoulder; tall cylindrical neck (wider at base); pinched spout; rim folded out and over; handle has two loops, one above the other; base concave. Decoration on each face, bordered by dots on three sides (not top): (1) two-handled jug with triangular base; (2) two triangles above each other with circular depression below; (3) possibly a schematic palm tree; (4) lozenge with four dots in the corners; (5) possibly a human figure; (6) unidentifiable.

Bibliography: Barag 1971: 48–49, fig. 37, Class C IV.
Parallels: Barag 1971: fig. 38 (Beth Shearim).

135. Pilgrim Jar

Probably Jerusalem
Byzantine Period, late 6th–7th cents. CE
Glass: mold-blown and intaglio decoration
Ht. 7.9 cm., width 7.2 cm.
Provenance unknown
From the Benguiat Collection   S 242

Description: hexagonal body with rounded shoulder; low, widely flaring neck, rim folded out and over; base slightly concave with swirl lines radiating from central incised circle. Intaglio design on six faces, each bordered by depressed dots: (1) *menorah* with tripod base; (2) unidentified x-shaped element with leaves on tips and horizontal bar across middle; (3) two concentric lozenges with pear-shaped depressions in each corner; (4) two concentric lozenges with third outer lozenge composed of depressed dots and four semi-circles in corners; (5) empty archway with column bases and capitals; (6) palm tree. Dark brown glass.

Bibliography: Barag 1970: 57:Class B V.
Parallels: Barag 1970: 56–57:Class V:1–10.

136. Stamp, Possibly for Bread

Possibly Northern Israel or Eastern Syria
Late Roman or Early Byzantine Periods, 4th–7th
 cent. CE
Bronze: cast
Ht. 5.5 cm., width 4.2 cm., depth 3.2 cm.
Purchased in Rome, said to come from Baghdad
Loaned by Mr. and Mrs. Norbert Schimmel L1982–3.7

Four stamps identical to this piece are known in the world, and it can be presumed that they were all made from the same mold. The symbolism on the stamp is the typical grouping of Temple and holyday ritual objects: the seven-branched *menorah*, the *shofar*, the incense shovel, and the *lulav*.

This stamp has been interpreted as used on bread, possibly to guarantee its ritual purity or to identify the baker (Meyers and Meyers 1975: 155). The *hallah* bread eaten on the Sabbath can only be pronounced ritually fit if it has been made from one of the five allowable species of grain, and if the required portion of the dough has been set aside for the priests (this is still set aside and burned today).

Description: rectangular face with central seven-branched *menorah*, arms curved and made of series of rectangles, tripod base, outer legs right-angled with bent feet; to left a *shofar*, to right a horseshoe-shaped implement with handle (probably a shovel) and above, a long thin object, probably a *lulav;* ring attached to back, with sub-rectangular knob on top.
Bibliography: Meyers and Meyers 1975.
Parallels: Reifenberg 1939: pl. 35:2; *Goodenough III:* figs. 1014,1017.

137. Oil Lamp

Southern Israel
Early–Middle Roman Period, 1st–2nd cent. CE
Clay: mold-formed, applied handle, knife-pared, fired
Length 10.2 cm., diam. 6.9 cm.
Purchased in Israel
Gift of the Betty and Max Ratner Collection   1981–89

Shortly after the destruction of the Second Temple in Jerusalem, the wheel-made "Herodian" forms with fan-shaped nozzles (see no. 103) began to appear in mold-made versions with relief decoration. The technique and use of decoration were influenced by Roman lamps (see no. 104). The motifs chosen were based on either religious or agricultural objects. The two globular objects on this lamp would appear to be stylized representations of pomegranates, a fruit that was brought to the Temple during *Shavuot,* the spring festival of the First Fruits. However, this identification is problematical, since a close parallel for the motifs on this lamp, including the design on the nozzle, represents our globular striped "pomegranates" in a more elongated form with curled handles. They have therefore been interpreted as jugs. In general, vertical striations seem to be reserved for jugs and amphorae, while pomegranates are solid with three triangular pieces coming off the top.

The other representation on the nozzle of our lamp is probably the bottom of a device which has been interpreted as a bird trap. The lamp with parallel decoration to ours mentioned above also depicts a bird caught in a trap.

Description: round bowl with carinated profile; top flat, fill hole and shoulder surrounded by thin raised ridge; fan-shaped nozzle with flat top and volutes on the sides; low ring base; vertical lug handle with notch on each side. Decoration consists of two globular, vertically striped objects, possibly pomegrantes, on the shoulder, and the remains of a design on the nozzle: a horizontal bar with three solid rectangles along its length and traces of a vertical shaft rising from midpoint with two arches.
Bibliography: Kozloff 1978: no. 46, fig. 53 center.
Parallels: Sussman 1970: no. 29; 1972: no. 71.

135

137

133

138. Jug
Israel
Middle Bronze II B, 1750–1550 BCE
Clay: wheel-turned, slipped, burnished, fired
Ht. 19.1 cm., diam. 7.3 cm.
Purchased in Israel
Gift of the Betty and Max Ratner
  Collection 1981–52

139. Carinated Bowl
Israel
Middle Bronze II B, 1750–1550 BCE
Clay: wheel-turned, slipped, fired
Ht. 8.4 cm., diam. 12.6 cm.
Purchased in Israel
Gift of the Betty and Max Ratner
  Collection 1981–53

140. Oil Lamp
Tell Ajjul
Middle Bronze Age, 2200–1550 BCE
Clay: wheel-turned, slipped, fired
Ht. 4.7 cm., diam. 13 cm.
Archaeology Acquisition Fund
  JM 12–73.36

141. Duck-bill Axe Head
Israel
Middle Bronze II B, 1750–1550 BCE
Bronze: cast
Length 9.9 cm., width 4.8 cm.
Purchased in Israel
Gift of the Betty and Max Ratner
  Collection 1981–214

142. Dagger Blade
Israel
Middle Bronze II B, 1750–1550 BCE
Bronze: cast
Length 17 cm., width 4.7 cm.
Purchased in Israel
Gift of the Betty and Max Ratner
  Collection 1981–221

143. Amphoriskos
Israel
Late Bronze II, 1400–1200 BCE
Clay: wheel-turned, slipped, burnished, painted, fired
Ht. 22 cm., diam. 17.5 cm.
Purchased in Israel
Gift of the Betty and Max Ratner
  Collection 1981–110

144. Stirrup Jar
Greece
Mycenaean III A, 1400–1300 BCE
Clay: wheel-turned, slipped, painted, fired
Ht. 11.5 cm., diam. 11.5 cm.
Purchased in Israel, said to come from near Hebron
Gift of the Betty and Max Ratner
  Collection 1981–159

145. Jug (*Bilbil*)
Cyprus
Late Bronze II, 1400–1200 BCE
Clay: hand-formed, slipped, fired
Ht. 14.8 cm., diam. 7 cm.
Purchased in Israel, said to come from near Hebron
Gift of the Betty and Max Ratner
  Collection 1981–161

146. Oil Lamp
Israel
Late Bronze II, 1400–1200 BCE
Clay: wheel-turned, slipped, fired
Ht. 6.3 cm., diam. 15.8 cm.
Purchased in Israel
Gift of the Betty and Max Ratner
  Collection 1981–109

147. Dagger Blade
Israel
Late Bronze I– II A, 1550–1300 BCE
Bronze: cast
Length 32 cm., width 4.1 cm.
Provenance unknown
Loaned by Daniel M. Friedenberg
  L1982–3.2

148. Pitcher
Israel
Iron II C, 800–586 BCE
Clay: wheel-turned, rolled handle, fired
Ht. 23.6 cm., diam. 16.3 cm.
Purchased in Israel, 1981
Gift of the Betty and Max Ratner
  Collection 1982–18

149. Plate with Spiral Burnish
Israel
Iron II C, 800–586 BCE
Clay: wheel-turned, slipped, burnished, fired
Ht. 4.1 cm., diam. 18.7 cm.
Purchased in Israel, 1981
Gift of the Betty and Max Ratner
  Collection 1982–7

150. Oil Lamp
Lachish, Tomb 106
Iron II C, 800–586 BCE
Clay: wheel-turned, slipped, fired
Ht. 5.2 cm., diam. 11.9 cm.
Archaeology Acquisition Fund
  JM 12–73.31

151. Toggle Pin for Clothing
Israel
Iron I, 1200–1000 BCE
Bronze: cast and hammered
Length 12.4 cm., diam. 0.7 cm.
Purchased in Israel
Gift of the Betty and Max Ratner
  Collection 1981–219

152. Horse Figurine
Israel
Iron II A–C, 1000–586 BCE
Clay: hand-formed and incised
Ht. 10 cm., width 3.8 cm., length 15.1 cm.
Purchased in Israel
Gift of the Betty and Max Ratner
  Collection 1981–223

153. Pilgrim Flask
Israel
Persian Period, 539–332 BCE
Clay: wheel-turned, applied wheel-turned neck, pre-pulled handles, slipped, fired
Ht. 28.2 cm., diam. 20.7 cm.
Purchased in Israel
Gift of the Betty and Max Ratner
  Collection 1981–150

154. Oil Lamp
Lachish, Tomb 109
Iron II C–Persian Period,
  600–550 BCE
Clay: slab-made (?), slipped, fired
Ht. 3.8 cm., diam. 12.5 cm.
Archaeology Acquisition Fund
  JM 12–73.60

155. Cosmetic Palette and Pestle
Israel
Persian Period, 5th cent. BCE
Alabaster: chiseled and ground
Ht. 2.1 cm., diam. 11.3 cm.
Purchased in Israel
Gift of the Betty and Max Ratner
  Collection 1981–213A,B

156. Spindle Bottle
Eastern Mediterranean
Late Hellenistic Period, 2nd–1st cent. BCE
Clay: wheel-turned, slipped, burnished,
  fired
Ht. 12.6 cm., diam. 3.6 cm.
Purchased in Israel, 1981
Gift of the Betty and Max Ratner
  Collection   1982–28

157. Cooking Pot
Israel
Late Hellenistic Period, 2nd–early
  1st cent. BCE
Clay: wheel-turned, pulled handles,
  fired
Ht. 14.5 cm., diam. 16.7 cm.
Purchased in Israel
Gift of the Betty and Max Ratner
  Collection   1981–94

158. Alabastron
Eastern Mediterranean
Late Hellenistic Period,
  2nd–1st cent. BCE
Glass: core-formed, marvered, thread
  handles
Ht. 12.5 cm., diam. 3.8 cm.
Purchased in Israel
Gift of the Betty and Max Ratner
  Collection   1981–125

**159. Figurine Head,
probably of a Female**
Cyprus (?)
Late Archaic Period, first half of
  the 5th cent. BCE
Limestone: carved and painted
Ht. 11.3 cm., width 7.1 cm.,
  depth 5.5 cm.
Purchased in Israel
Gift of the Betty and Max Ratner
  Collection   1981–129

160. Trefoil-mouth Pitcher
Eastern Mediterranean
Late Roman Period, 4th cent. BCE
Glass: free-blown, thread handle
  and decoration
Ht. 23.2 cm., diam. 14.3 cm.
Purchased in Israel
Gift of Judith Riklis   1981–296

**161. Oil Lamp with Olive Leaf
Design**
Israel
Early–Middle Roman Period,
  1st–2nd cent. CE
Clay: mold-formed, slipped, fired
Ht. 2.9 cm., diam. 6.6 cm.
Purchased in Israel
Gift of the Betty and Max Ratner
  Collection   1981–90

162. Cooking Pot
Israel
Middle Roman–Early Byzantine Period,
  2nd–6th cent. CE
Clay: wheel-turned, pulled handles,
  slipped, fired
Purchased in 1940,
  said to come from Caesarea
S 1206

163. Candlestick Unguentarium
Eastern Mediterranean
Middle Roman Period, late
  2nd–3rd cent. CE
Glass: free-blown
Ht. 16.3 cm., diam. 4.9 cm.
Purchased in Israel
Gift of the Betty and Max Ratner
  Collection   1981–81

164. Globular Jar
Eastern Mediterranean
Late Roman Period, 3rd–4th cent. CE
Glass: free-blown and wheel-incised
Ht. 14.2 cm., diam. 9 cm.
Purchased in Israel
Gift of Judith Riklis   1981–267

165. Two-handled Flask
Eastern Mediterranean
Late Roman Period, 3rd–4th cent. CE
Glass: free-blown, spiraled,
  thread handles
Ht. 10.9 cm., width 6.7 cm.
Purchased in Israel
Gift of the Betty and Max Ratner
  Collection   1981–74

166. Trefoil-mouth Pitcher
Eastern Mediterranean
Late Roman Period, 3rd–4th cent. CE
Glass: free-blown, thread handle and
  decoration
Ht. 12.8 cm., diam. 7.7 cm.
Purchased in Israel
Gift of Judith Riklis   1981–295

167. Storage Jar
Khirbet el-Kom (Israel)
Iron II C, 800–586 BCE
Clay: wheel-turned, pulled handles,
  fired, drilled
Ht. 46.7 cm., diam. 30.1 cm.
Loaned by the Hebrew Union College
Skirball Museum, Los Angeles   A/758

168. Bangle
Lachish, Tomb 116
Iron II B–C, 900–586 BCE
Bronze: cast
Diam. 9.95 cm., diam. of cross section
  1.6 cm., wt. 367 gms.
Archaeology Acquisition Fund
  JM 12–73.430

169. Sling Shot (?)
Tell Ajjul, findspot unknown
Date undetermined
Clay: hand-formed and baked
Ht. 4.3 cm.
Archeology Acquisition Fund
  JM 12–73.305

170. Sling Shot (?)
Tell Ajjul, find spot unknown
Date undetermined
Clay: hand-formed and baked
Diam. 5.2 cm.
Archaeology Acquisition Fund
  JM 12–73.269

**171. Replica of Lachich Letter III
Mentioning a Prophet**
Lachish, Level II, Gate Room E.18C
Iron II C, ca. 586 BCE
Clay: fired and inked
Original in Israel Museum   PM 38.127
Replica courtesy of the Israel Museum

**172. Replica of Lachish Letter IV
Mentioning the Signals of
Lachish and Azekah**
Lachish, Level II, Gate Room E.18C
Iron II C, ca. 586 BCE
Clay: fired and inked
Original in the Israel Museum
  PM 38.128
Replica courtesy of the Israel Museum

**173. Replica of Lachish Letter VI
Mentioning Military Orders from
Jerusalem**
Lachish, Level II, Gate Room E.18C
Iron II C, ca. 586 BCE
Clay: fired and inked
Original in the Israel Museum,
  PM 38.129
Replica courtesy of the Israel Museum

**174. Stamp Seal with
Worshipper Before the Altar of
the Babylonian God Marduk**
Mesopotamia (Iraq)
Neo-Babylonian Period, 6th–5th cent. BCE
Chalcedony: carved, drilled, incised;
  handle: bronze wire, twisted
Ht. of seal 2.9 cm., width 1.5 cm.,
  length 2.2 cm.
Loaned by Daniel M. Friedenberg
  L1982-3.6

175. Cylinder Seal with Worshipper before Scorpion Man
Mesopotamia (Iraq)
Neo-Babylonian Period, 7th–5th cent. BCE
Lapis lazuli: carved and drilled
Ht. 2.5 cm., diam. 1.25 cm.
Provenance unknown
Loaned by the Metropolitan Museum
   of Art   Bequest of W. Gedney Beatty,
   1941   41.160.320

176. Duck-shaped Stamp Seal with Representation of Worshipper
Mesopotamia (Iraq)
Neo-Assyrian or Neo-Babylonian
   Period, 7th–6th cent. BCE
Chalcedony: carved and drilled
Ht. 1.8 cm., width 1.4 cm., length 2.5 cm.
Purchased in Israel
Gift of the Betty and Max Ratner
   Collection   1981–130

177. Replica of the Cylinder of King Cyrus of Persia Allowing Exiles in Babylon to Return to Their Homelands
Original cylinder:
Persia (Iran)
Achaemenid Period, ca. 539 BCE
Clay: inscribed and fired
Ht. 23.3 cm., diam. 9.8 cm.
Inscription in Babylonian Akkadian
commemorates the conquering of the
Babylonians.
Portions of the original in the British
Museum   BM 90980 and the Yale
   Babylonian Collection   NBC 2504
Cast courtesy of the Yale Babylonian
   Collection

178. Replica of a *Puru* Text, Mentioning the Custom of Casting Lots
Original *puru:*
Mesopotamia (Iraq)
Neo-Assyrian Period, 824 BCE
Clay: inscribed and fired
Ht. 2.6 cm., width 2.6 cm., depth 2.6 cm.
Akkadian inscription of Ihali, Grand
   Vizier to King Shalmaneser III of Assyria
Original in the Yale Babylonian
   Collection   YBC 7058
Cast courtesy of the Yale Babylonian
   Collection

179. Daric (Coin)
Persia (Iran)
Achaemenid Period, 5th cent. BCE
Gold: stamped
Diam. 1.5 cm., wt. 8.5 gms.
Provenance unknown
Gift of Samuel Friedenberg   U 7176

180. Eastern Sigillata Ware Bowl
Beth Shan, Level II, House III sub
Early Roman Period, 30 BCE–70 CE
Clay: wheel-turned, slipped, fired
Ht. 5.2 cm., diam. 15.9 cm.
Loaned by the University Museum,
   University of Pennsylvania   29–102–542

181. Western Sigillata Ware Plate
Cologne
Early to Middle Roman Period,
   probably 1st–2nd cent. CE
Clay: wheel-turned, incised, slipped,
   fired
Ht. 7.5 cm., diam. 29 cm.
Ex. Balz Collection
Loaned by the Newark Museum,
   The Eugene Schaefer
   Collection   50.170

182. Replica of an Oil Lamp with Representation of *Menorah, Shofar, Lulav* and *Etrog*
Original lamp:
Eastern Mediterranean
Late Roman–Early Byzantine Periods,
   4th–6th cent. CE
Bronze: cast and incised
Ht. 10.9 cm., width 9.2 cm., length 17.5 cm.
Original in the Mizyam Shaar
   Schloessinger Collection, New York
Cast gift of Dr. Harry G. Friedman
   F5736

183. *Shofar* (Ram's Horn)
Israel
20th cent. CE
Ram's horn: hollowed
Diam. 7.5 cm.
Purchased in Israel
Loaned by Mr. and Mrs. Nash
   Aussenberg   L1982–3.14